The Camper's and Backpacker's Bible

Tom Huggler

Drawings by Ed Sutton

DOUBLEDAY
NEW YORK LONDON TORONTO SYDNEY AUCKLAND

PUBLISHED BY DOUBLEDAY
a division of Bantam Doubleday Dell Publishing Group, Inc.
1540 Broadway, New York, New York 10036

DOUBLEDAY and the portrayal of an anchor with a dolphin
are trademarks of Doubleday, a division of Bantam
Doubleday Dell Publishing Group, Inc.

Library of Congress Cataloging-in-Publication Data

Huggler, Thomas E.
  The camper's and backpacker's bible./ Tom Huggler:
drawings by Ed Sutton
      p.   cm.
  ISBN 0-385-47194-7
  1. Camping—Equipment and supplies.
  2. Backpacking—Equipment and supplies..   I. Title.
GV191.76.H84   1995
796.54—dc20   94-24426
                                    CIP

July 1995

10   9   8   7   6   5   4   3   2   1

First Edition

To my mother, Leona C. Huggler,
who left the porch light on and
the door unlocked, in case we boys had
camped enough for one summer night

ACKNOWLEDGMENTS

Writing may be a lonely business, but no one writes a book without the help of others.

Thanks, first, to my mother for encouraging me to follow the written word wherever it led.

Thanks to my wife, Laura, for taking to the trail with me and for offering constructive criticism with the text.

Contents

APPENDIX

INTRODUCTION

You were probably too young to remember now how you spread a blanket over living-room furniture to make your first crude tent. My mother says I was three, maybe four years old. It is easier to recall those youthful shelters built out-of-doors. Grade-school friends and I liked to find clumps of sumac because the dense canopy supported the bed sheets borrowed from Mother's clothesline. The sumac thickets hid us from the prying eyes of brothers and sisters who might also reveal why Dad's favorite flashlight suddenly reappeared—only slightly worse for wear—following my latest campout.

Except for their gray color, the thick sumac stems brought to mind bamboo, which made our jungle encampment beyond the backyard lawn all that much more realistic.

Mankind has been camping for thousands of years.

The kids' camps like those that you and I built became more sophisticated as we grew older. The day hikes turned into overnighters with canvas tarpaulins providing the shelter until that memorable Christmas day when we received the Official Boy Scout Pup Tent. Years later, the progression for some campers has lead all the way to an expensive Pace Arrow motorhome. But most of us who camped as kids and still love the sport are content to stuff a backpack with lightweight gear, stake down the family tent at a county campground, or tow our folding camping trailer through a national park. Maybe it's the knowledge that only a thin layer of canvas separates us from the canopy of stars.

An American Tradition

Campers, consciously or otherwise, connect with the land and its cultural history. For thousands of years nomadic peoples from Bedouin herders to Inuit hunters have relied on tent camps for shelter and community. Closer to home, the bark house of the Iroquois and the elk-hide tipi of the Sioux were no less a comfort than the bleached canvas of the prairie schooner. Lewis and Clark tented their way up the Missouri River from St. Louis and back down again two years later.

Camping on a bluff overlooking sparkling Lake Sakakawea in North Dakota, I felt the tug of history. No wonder so many of the nation's campgrounds, both public and private, are located near historic sites like Yellowstone and Mt. Rushmore. The roots of organized camping go back to 1861 when Frederick William Gunn, a boys' private school director in Connecticut, arranged for his students to spend the summer camping out, cooking and hiking. Gunn hoped the young men's thirst for adventure would be satisfied and they would return to school that fall and not enlist in the Union army.

By the time the American Camping Association was founded in 1910, camping as a recreational sport was well launched. Two early travelers out to capture the romantic gypsy lifestyle on the nation's improving road system were inventors Henry Ford and Thomas Edison. In 1916, the pair teamed with two other friends, naturalist John Burroughs and tire magnate Harvey Firestone, to travel and camp out of converted motorcars. The Vagabonds unwittingly paved the way for modern RVs because they had all the amenities of home, including electric lighting and a cook stove.

Americans began camping for fun in large numbers at the close of WW

"There is hardly an adult who does not long for the time when he can escape from the confining repressive environment of modern city civilization to the freedom and simplicity of the open road and the camp, or to some place he can call his own in the country." Those words, from the book *Camping Out: A Manual of Organized Camping*, are as true today as when they were written in 1924.

Growth in camping was especially strong between the two world wars, slowed during the Great Depression (although many families lived in tents by necessity), and exploded again after WW II. There is no sign that the peak has been reached.

Go back in time and you will learn that where there was a camp there was also fire. Campfires were the early communal bonds for our hunting and exploring ancestors. Gathered around the nightly flames, they shared the day's experiences, providing the original spark of oral tradition. Nearly 200 years ago, a campfire story was the genesis for 19-year-old Mary Shelley to write *Frankenstein*. The American tall tale has its roots in the flickering firelight of Eastern and Midwestern lumber camps and in Western wagon-train encampments.

Anyone who has not shared a ghost story around a campfire has missed an important part of growing up outdoors in America. Friends of mine own a small piece of land on northern Michigan's Manistee River. Every summer they set up a big war surplus tent for family and friends to use whenever they wish. On any summer evening you can watch a dozen children toast marshmallows over glowing campfire embers, while the adults relax in lawn chairs. Everyone goes home happy.

My generation has a nostalgic need to return to the simpler life of only 30 years ago when families took longer vacations (today, the average family vacation lasts only four days). That is why camping is growing so rapidly in popularity, and why—according to the U.S. Travel Data Center—it is now the second-most popular vacation activity. Hiking, incidentally, is first. And not all the campers are modern types. Some people actually enjoy "roughing it," dressing in buckskins, cooking over open fires, and sleeping in traditional frontier-style tents.

Who Camps?

So add camping and hiking to the list of Great American Love Affairs that counts automobiles, sports, and rock and roll among its passions. If you're not included in the estimated one-fourth to one-third of all Americans who in a typical year pound tent stakes or park their RV overnight next to a picnic table somewhere in the outdoors, the question is, "Why not?" Two-thirds of heads of households surveyed by the University of Michigan agreed that camping is the best vacation a family can take.

According to the National Sporting Goods Association, about 49 million Americans backpacked or camped in wilderness in 1992, an increase of 7 million in only four years.

Campers and backpackers come from all walks of life, and the campground itself is the common denominator. Your neighbor might be a college professor, a laid-off auto worker, a retired pharmacist or a Boy Scout working on a merit badge. Recently I interviewed a woman who told me she went camping before she was born because her parents weren't about to let a pregnancy get in the way of their annual outdoors vacation. The oldest camper I recall meeting was 94; his wife was 91. They shared with me plans for their next outing.

Why Camp?

There are many reasons why people go camping. First, the sport is afford-able. The average nightly campground fee is about $14, much less than a motel or hotel room. Second, camping brings families together for a unique shared experience—the reason why 90 percent of university survey respon-dents said they planned to vacation in the first place. Third, more and more people are becoming interested in the environment. What better way to understand and help the natural world than by participating as a camper?

Camping is as American as baseball and hotdogs. Some modern campers take a traditional approach to the sport.

Many of us avid sportsmen were introduced to the outdoors through family camping vacations, via Scouting adventures, or some other organized activity for youths. For more than forty years camping has been my path to outdoor sport throughout North America and in other lands. As a hunter and fisherman, camping has allowed me flexibility in pursuit of game and fish, and it has added immeasurably to the satisfaction of those activities. Camping has strengthened bonds with my family, it has helped me stretch vacation dollars, and it has allowed me to meet interesting people and make lifelong friends. I cannot imagine a world without camping.

Close your eyes and imagine the aroma of pine pitch. Now woodsmoke. Now leather. These smells are among those that even our blunted olfactories instantly associate with outdoor sport. For campers, nothing rivals the smell of new-stretched canvas. Korean manufacturers of synthetic-fabric tents could probably double sales by spraying the technicolor interiors with parfum de canvas.

Everyone loves a tent. Recently at an outdoor show I watched two older sportsmen stroll into a big army tent that one of the exhibitors had erected. One of the men filled his lungs with a deep breath, sighed, and exhaled noisily. "Ahhhhh!" he exclaimed. "Now I can make it another year." Then he and his friend began to swap fond memories of their camping experiences.

The Importance of Attitude

Not every night outdoors, however, is so pleasant. I well remember a summer thunderstorm that mildly panicked my wife and me. Continuous lightning flashes brightened the woods like a battery of arc welders. The nonstop clap and crack of thunder had us wondering if the combined battles of Bull Run were any more bone-jarring. Confined to our little backpacking tent, we breathed the new-mown hay smell of ozone and hoped the next tree to go down would not drop on us.

Many people shudder at the thought of pitching a tent because they view nature as unkind, even dangerous. Afraid of insects, snakes and wild animals, these people also have a fear of the dark and the woods and the unknown. Forced to spend a night outdoors, they singe themselves by getting too close to the campfire, and they don't sleep well—if at all.

Others might have had a bad experience outdoors. Campers who have gotten cold, wet or dirty in the past can hardly be blamed for never wanting to unroll another sleeping bag. A skunk in the tent is a turn-off that can last a lifetime. Who wants their privacy invaded by a noisy motorcycle gang in full regalia? And who prays their sleep will be interrupted by the distractions of a lumpy bed, blood-sucking mosquitoes, or hard-rock music from the neighbor's blaring radio?

The way past these and other nuisance problems begins with a positive attitude. That's because the beginning camper who expects to experience a lousy time outdoors will get his or her wish. Instead, prepare for—make that "plan for"—the temporary aggravations of sand on the tent floor, the passing thunderstorm that stayed a bit too long, the midnight raid by a raccoon attracted to the campground dumpster. So what if you make hash-blacked potatoes because you're not used to cooking with propane? You'll only do it once, and you'll learn from the experience.

Although it is possible to take the amenities of home along with you—portable satellite dish, hair dryer, microwave—these are the modern conveniences that rob most campers of the whole point of living outdoors for a little while. Too much of the indoors brought outdoors destroys the fun experiences of starwatching on a clear night or cooking over an open fire like the pioneers did. No one ever became a good camper without experience; if you're open to learning, the pesky problems can be fun, especially in retrospect.

We go for the outdoor experience, good or bad, but—the way I figure it—always better than the flickering television from some motel room. As common and sometimes frustrating as camping can be, the sport offers intangible rewards. Near Mio one summer evening years ago, I introduced my young son to brook trout fishing and, later that same night, to the piercing call of a whippoorwill perched on a limb over our tent.

Freshly divorced, I wanted to give my son and his younger sister a taste of family adventure outdoors. So we made annual treks to an island in Lake Huron, and one summer traveled 9,000 miles during a long camping trip to the West where I developed an addiction to hobo pies and s'mores.

An old Coleman tent I used over those years and recently sold at rummage for $30 saved me nearly $4,000 in motel bills. Not every trip was a joy, but each was memorable. Atop a mountain in British Columbia, for example, my son and I shared a damp sleeping bag when his got soaked in a sleet storm. "I don't think I want to go camping anymore, Dad." he said.

Another time, after being drowned out of a state park during an incessant summer rain, the kids and I found ourselves watching *Bronco Billy*, surely the worst movie Clint Eastwood ever made, at a theater in town. "I *know* I never want to camp again," my daughter insisted.

Things change. Last summer my son borrowed gear to take his own family on a camping trip. My college-student daughter's goal is to backpack and camp her way across Australia. Camping is now in their blood, too.

I

CHOOSING THE RIGHT GEAR

If you've never camped or maybe just haven't unrolled a sleeping bag in years, you'll be surprised—maybe stunned is a better way to put it—at the gear options. Compact, lightweight tents stay dry, are durable, never need to be re-waterproofed, and set up in minutes—with no need for an engineering degree. Lightweight sleeping bags are warm, and state-of-the-art mattress pads are comfortable. Stoves as small as one-pound capacity coffee cans light in all weather conditions (sometimes without matches!) and burn for hours. Backpacks ease, if not eliminate, the strain of carrying heavy loads long distances.

Camping gear need not be expensive although, like anything else, it can be. According to a recent survey by *Sports Trend* magazine, the average best-selling price point for a tent was $84.32; for a sleeping bag, $36.42. Adding a basic sleeping pad, stove and lantern will bump your investment to $200 or so. But the $50 or more per night you'll save on a motel means you can pay for your camping equipment within a few days of use. With the dollars you can save by shopping around for good prices you could buy a small backpack.

I use the term "investment" because, when properly cared for, camp-

1

Gear choices for backpackers and campers have exploded thanks to competition among manufacturers and the discovery of strong, lightweight synthetic materials.

ing equipment will last many years, and it has many applications. Sleeping bags for the kids are useful for TV lounging and slumber parties and serve as a hedge in drafty college dormitories. That campstove and lantern you store in the attic may come in handy during a power outage emergency. Take them, along with your tent, on your next business trip or travel vacation. If the motels are full, you'll have an option to consider.

You never know when camping gear will come in handy. A few years ago, three of us were hunting on the Alaska Peninsula when bad weather forced us to land our float plane on a tundra lake. The lightweight

Most of the equipment in this photo (fluorescent lantern, portable shower, 3 1/2-pound tent, windproof and breathable sleeping bag) has only recently been available.

When properly cared for, camping gear will last many years. This tent and stove have seen years of service.

tent that one of my partners had thoughtfully remembered to pack provided temporary shelter until the skies cleared. Without that shelter we would have been miserable.

What should you buy and how much should you pay for it? Before making any purchase, consider how much and under what conditions you expect to need the equipment. A lightweight sleeping bag, for example, might be fine for flatlands summer camping but a poor choice for the mountains or that outing you plan for next fall.

You may not want to buy anything at first, nor do you have to. Some sporting goods stores and campgrounds rent camping gear (look under "Camping Equipment—Renting" in the *Yellow Pages* of your telephone directory), or perhaps you can borrow from a friend or neighbor until deciding what you need. Another option is to check out used stuff. Flea markets, rummage sales, pawn shops, army/navy surplus outlets, and various other second-hand stores are great places to find bargains. Running a want-to-buy classified ad in the local paper could turn up other deals for you.

When you do buy, look for value, quality and—if purchasing used gear—condition. More on that in a moment.

TENTS

The need for shelter is about as elemental as our basic requirements for food and safety. Tenting is probably encoded in our genes by now, or ever since Cro-Magnon wandered from the cave and stretched a wooly mammoth hide to protect him from wild beasts and the elements.

When I was a kid, we camped in nylon or poplin pup tents and mountain tents. Once in awhile we dragged out the heavy canvas tents our fathers or grandfathers had used and stored away in the attic. A look through an old Abercrombie Camp Outfitters catalog helps me to identify the old specialty tents: Explorer, Cruiser, Wedge, Miner's, Baker and Foresters, among others. Many people made their own tents from these and inventive other designs.

Backpacking Tents

Most of us no longer do that because nearly any kind of tent we might need is available and affordable. Consider the backpacking tent, a generic name for the new lightweight, carry-it-on-your-back models. In 1975, North Face introduced the Oval Invention, the first dome tent, and the world of geodesic design began. Ideal for one or two people, these backpacking tents use space-age synthetic materials to be lightweight and strong. They come in hexagonal, hoop, conestoga and various other geode-sic-domed shapes to make maximum use of roof lines although most feature just enough space for a couple of sleeping bags and a minimum amount of gear. Even though you can stretch in them, the roof lines in one- and two-person models arc too low for someone to stand erect. Better tents have sewn-in, tub-style floors and a waterproof rainfly.

To my mind, backpacking tents offer the widest range of potential

Freestanding backpacking tents in dome style make maximum use of space.

The North Face designed the first dome-style, lightweight tent. The two-person Cicada model features dual entrances and nearly vertical walls.

use. Small and light, they are easy to tote in canoe or floatplane, on a bicycle or in a backpack. They set up quickly and are handy for emergency shelter as well as a temporary home. At least two companies now make models that set up in 60 seconds or less. With a pull of a lanyard located at the peak, Camel's Sixty-Second Tent opens like a parachute. When thrown into the air, the Pop-Tent by Softsports, Inc. hits the ground fully assembled. These tents fold into a 2-inch-high circle about 40 inches in diameter for easy transportation and storage.

You can always find a backpacking tent in my truck, and I spend probably half of my nights outdoors sleeping in one type or another. Body heat alone will usually warm these small shelters, and that is why they are the choice of the winter camper.

Costs vary from $60 to $600 with the upper range reserved for expedition models that are designed for high mountain winds and extremely cold temperatures. Popular models and manufacturers of entry-level

Better camping and backpacking tents feature two-layer construction with removable rainfly.

The author found this Gander Mountain dome tent warm and comfortable for fall backpacking.

backpacking tents include Jansport, Eureka! (Johnson Camping) and Camel Outdoor Products. Among many specialty companies are North Face, Quest, Walrus, Kelty and Outbound (Taymore Industries). For the addresses of these and other manufacturers, consult the Appendix.

Family Tents

Family tents are larger and heavier than backpacking tents but are not necessarily more costly. Four-person family tents in dome, cottage, umbrella or cabin style are sometimes sale-priced at under $75 although it is possible to spend several hundred dollars, too. The less expensive ones are made mostly in the Orient, or at least their nylon, poplin and polyester fabrics are made there and then shipped to the U.S. for assembly. Popular brand names include Nelson/Weather-Rite, Coleman, Stansport and Gander Mountain.

The fabrics are not waterproof, however, and that is why some companies coat them with urethane or back the material with a waterproof membrane. Bibler tents are made from thinstretched Teflon laminated to nylon Ripstop. According to the manufacturer, the resulting Tod-dTex fabric is both totally waterproof and windproof, thus precluding the need for a rainfly.

Better built tents like Bibler and Moss models have sewn-in floors with tub-style sidewalls (the floor, usually constructed from vinyl or nylon taffeta, extends for several inches onto the walls). Seams are dou-

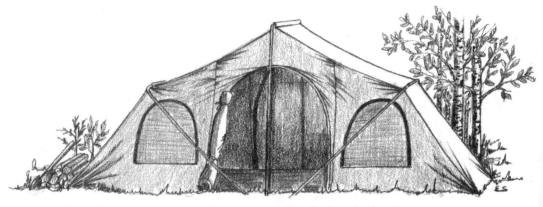

The cabin style is one of the most popular designs in family tents.

This umbrella-style tent from Eureka! comes with a rainfly and is large enough for adults to stand up in.

ble-stitched and waterproof-coated. Zippers are heavy-duty, and there are plenty of windows with fine-mesh screening to keep out insects. Aluminum or fiberglass poles are standard these days, and most manufacturers employ some type of shock cord system for putting the poles together. Check tubular materials for strength—more-reputable companies use tempered aluminum instead of fiberglas. Know, too, that tent pegs are often a tip-off to quality. Thin, soft-metal ones are usually cheap. Wooden or plastic pegs are better, but they are also heavier.

Inspect the tent erected before buying. The tent itself and rainfly should be drum-tight, and the rainfly should completely cover the tent and stake to the ground. Extra loops for securing the structure in a storm, a storm-proof vestibule, and mesh pockets along the sides and a dome net for storing gear are other quality features to look for.

My wife and I rely on a four-person model when using our vehicle for destination camping. Although we prefer sleeping in smaller backpacking tents, we also set up the family tent for storing gear and to use as a changing room.

Many modern tents are so affordable that some parents buy a second one for the kids, giving them their own space and Mom and Dad some privacy.

Perfect for summer camping, family tents see service in spring and fall, too, but will likely need to be heated then. That can create a problem when burning fossil fuels, especially overnight, because the tents are not designed for stovepipe ventilation. So I'll often rely on a small propane-fired catalytic heater for five minutes or so, just enough time to remove a morning chill. Even then, however, I'm careful to zip open a window for ventilation.

Wall Tents

Wall tents are the first choice of serious anglers and hunters and family campers who operate for days or weeks at a time out of a destination camp. Wall tents feature sidewall construction and an internal ridge pole, and they range in size from 8 feet by 10 feet to 16 feet by 32 feet. Equipped with stovepipe jacks, the tents are heated with wood, oil, propane or coal. Fully equipped ones often contain a pantry, kitchen sink, stove with oven, and built-in bunks and storage cabinets. Army surplus tents, especially those that saw duty as cook shacks (usually dark colored, these are well-preserved from cooking oils and smoke) are always popular.

Cotton-duck canvas from 7 oz. to 18 oz. per yard is used to manufacture most wall tents and frontiersman or tipi-style tents. Montana Canvas offers a 7 oz. polyester it calls Genesis, and the Polaris from San Antonio Tent is constructed of 50/50 cotton duck and polyester. When buying cotton-duck canvas, check to make sure the material is treated with a waterproofing sealant (marine duck canvas is treated with chemicals to be waterproof). To do the job yourself, buy a quality sealant from a tent and awning supplier, then test a small part of the tent in an inconspicuous place to make sure the sealant doesn't damage or stain the fabric.

Most wall tents are made in this country, many in small cottage industries located in western states. Canvas Cabins, Mountain Cat and Salem Tent & Awning come to mind. Bigger companies to consider include Cabela's, Woods Canada Ltd., Montana Canvas and Colorado Tent. Prices range from $300 to $1,000 or more.

Tent Tips

A friend of mine is not happy with a new tent he bought last year. Corners of the tent leaked when it rained during his family's summer vacation. Erecting the shelter—if it can be called that—was an exercise in frustration because someone who didn't understand English wrote the directions. And the tent was too small for my friend's family of five. Whatever tent you buy, keep in mind the following considerations:

• Buy what you can afford, remembering that the more you use your new tent, the greater its potential value becomes.

• Tent design dictates everything. Floor space, ventilation, head clearance, overall size and—to some degree—weight and even price are determined by the tent's design.

• Practical uses. Wall tents offer all the comforts of home and make a beautiful permanent camp. On the other hand, family-style tents are great for vacations lasting from two days to two weeks. Smaller, less bulky models are fine for packing into a canoe or the car trunk. Consider a backpacking tent, though, when weight and space are factors or when a quick overnight shelter is needed.

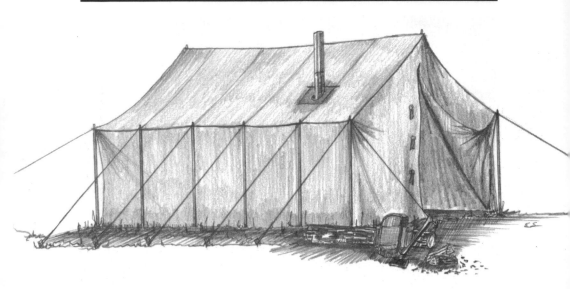

Wall tents are an American camping tradition. Although they're heavy and take time to set up, they make comfortable long-term camps.

The author photographed this wall tent in interior Alaska where it has seen service over many years.

Light-colored tents like this Quest model are cooler for summer camping. Note large openings for cross-ventilation.

• Four-season use. Thanks to their two-layer construction, most backpacking tents can be used year around. Specially designed ones feature snow valances, breather holes and adjustable vents to eliminate wind shear.

• Material types and colors. Light-colored fabrics allow better light penetration, but darker colors absorb more heat. Whatever you choose, make sure the fabric has been treated with a fire retardant.

• Other quality features. Look for bells and whistles, too. Mesh pockets for storing wallet, eyeglasses and other personal items will be appreciated. So are privacy curtains, skylights, full sidewall windows, D rings for hanging a pencil light, retractable clothesline, extra storage spots and built-in awnings.

• Easy up, easy down? With practice you should be able to set up a backpacking tent in five minutes or less, a family tent in about ten minutes. Wall tents require more time and additional manpower. Not only should any tent you buy be a cinch for a fifth grader to erect, all directions should be clearly illustrated.

• Buy used. A used tent may cost a fraction of a new model. Putting an ad in the local newspaper or scouting around the neighborhood for yard sales could result in a good deal. Before parting with your money, however, ask to inspect the erected tent. Check to see that all the parts are there, then examine the fabric for tears or holes. Run a garden hose over the roof and seams to make sure they don't leak.

SLEEPING PADS AND BAGS

Enjoyment of the outdoors always begins with a restful night's sleep. Think back to the last night you spent under the stars. Did you wake up tired with a trip-hammer headache and sore muscles? Or did you emerge refreshed and ready to face a great day outdoors?

Unless the weather is foul, most campers don't spend unnecessary time in the sack. The quality of sleep, therefore, is more important than the number of hours spent in repose. To get it, buy a sleeping system that works for you. Begin by choosing the right sleeping pad and bag.

Sleeping Pads

Patio lounge chairs are fine for capturing a tan but are lousy to sleep on for more than an hour or two. Cots are equally confining although they beat snoozing on the bare ground. Goode Products, Byer of Maine and Sierra Corporation make high-quality cots with mattresses. I love to sleep on a spongelike, four-inch foam pad of open-cell construction, but such pads are bulky to transport in car or truck. Too bad it's not a perfect world.

The Therm-A-Rest from Cascade Designs is a foam pad that self-inflates.

Some campers and backpackers can get by with a ¹/₂-inch-thick pad of denser, closed-cell foam. Because I can't, I often tote a 1¹/₂-inch-thick pad that contains 1¹/₄ inches of open-cell foam and ¹/₄ inch of Ensolite, a dense closed-cell product. Foam Design Consumer Products (Blue Ridge Pads) and C/H Manufacturing Co. (Frelonic and High Country Pads) are two of several companies making foam pads from $10 to $40.

Air mattresses are okay if you inflate them just enough to keep your tailbone from touching the ground, but most campers overinflate their air mattresses and sleep poorly as a result. The inflatables are also noisy. Wonderful options on today's market include the Therm-A-Rest pad from Cascade Designs, which mates open-cell foam with a self-inflating air mattress. I've found mine to be light in weight, compact in size when rolled up, and extremely comfortable. Other companies making similar pads, which cost upwards of $50, are Slumberjack and Gymwell.

A few companies make cushioned seats, which double as sleeping pads. Hammocks are another consideration, and are actually a necessity when camping in the Tropics.

Gone are the days when campers had to cut pine boughs for their mattress and dig hip holes in the ground. Today's environmentally conscious camper doesn't subscribe to those destructive practices. Thanks to good gear, he doesn't have to.

Sleeping Bags

Unlike home furnaces, which can be measured in Btu's of heat, there is no industry standard for sleeping bags. Most companies use an arbitrary rating system, which is keyed to the number of pounds of insula-

Today's flyweight tent, sleeping bag and pad fit snugly into a light pack. Total weight: 15 to 20 pounds.

Sleeping bag manufacturers are always trying to insulate their products with improved materials. Thinsulate Lite Loft insulation from 3M is lighter in weight than continuous filament polyester and 7-hole premium polyester (top row). It is also more compressible (middle row) and provides more loft (bottom row).

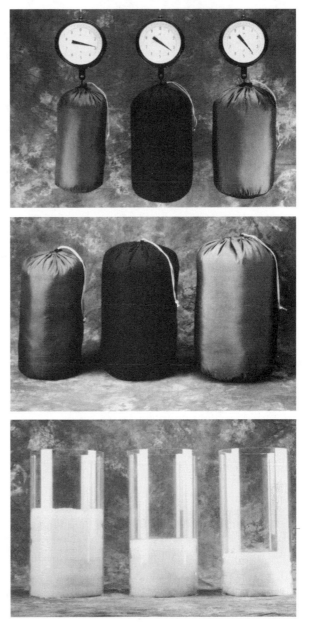

tion in their products. The information is valuable, therefore, only in understanding that company's product line.

Typically, however, a 1- to 2-pound lightweight bag, is rated to 40 degrees F.; a medium-weight (2 1/2 to 3 pounds of fill) to 25 or 30 degrees; a heavyweight (4 pounds) to zero or 10 degrees; and an expedition-weight (five or six pounds) to well below zero. To be sure you get a sleeping bag warm enough for you, discount the manufacturer's rating system by at least 10 degrees. In other words, you might reasonably expect a 20-degree bag to keep you warm at 30 degrees and above.

It isn't that the companies are lying. Individual metabolism, what you have eaten or drunk, what you wear to bed, and tent type and location are other factors that determine warmth and comfort.

Keep in mind, too, that the sleeper warms the bag; the bag does not warm the sleeper. The bag's purpose is to slow the loss of body heat through convection (movement and escape of air within the bag) and conduction (transfer from your body to the ground). Another truth: When blood circulation slows during sleep, heat rises to the body torso, and extremities—head, feet and hands—cool. That is also why the old trapper and lumberjack maxim of wearing a woolen cap to bed is still a sensible idea when sleeping outdoors in cold weather. Socks and gloves may help, too.

Down or Synthetic?

Goose down offers more insulation for its weight and bulk than do synthetic fibers such as Hollofil, PrimaLoft, and PolarGuard HV. Thus, a 3-pound down model may be equivalent to a 5- or 6-pound synthetic. Natural down is wonderful, but it is considerably more expensive and

Kelty's Soft Touch sleeping bags contain Thinsulate Lite Loft and come in mummy style for men (left) and women.

may not even be needed. Further, when down becomes wet, it loses its loft, which is a material's ability to fluff up and hold heat. The amount of loft in a sleeping bag, regardless of fill type, can vary from 2 to 9 inches. Tip: Shaking out the bag and allowing it to air out each morning helps restore loft.

Manmade materials have come a long way since the Kapok-filled bags of my Scouting youth. Today's factory insulations are lighter and warmer than ever, and many are durable enough to withstand repeated washings. Although not waterproof, a few are water-resistant. Those featuring continuous-filament fibers tend to loft very well.

Product availability is strong these days with some 50 companies making sleeping bags. Standard size is 33 inches wide and 75 inches long, but models are now available for pint-sized kid campers to big sportsmen who stand 6 feet 8 inches tall. Many of these bags are reasonably priced, too. Wenzel, for example, makes a line of products it calls its Oversize bags—38 inches wide to 81 inches long—with prices starting at only $47.

Use Considerations

But how much do you want to spend for a good night's rest? Sleeping bags run the price gamut from $20 slumber party lightweights to $600 for a goose down polar-weight model. Hollofil II and Quallofil insula-

Two different bags, each rated for 20 degrees, are made by Slumberjack. At 3 pounds, 13 ounces, the rectangular-cut Quest is only 3 ounces heavier than the mummy-style Conquest sleeping bag.

tions are less expensive than some of the newer synfills such as Micro-loft and Lite Loft. As you ponder the options, keep in mind, too, that how a sleeping bag is constructed is as important as the material inside.

To illustrate: A mummy-shaped bag with sculpted head protector and drawstring will be much warmer (and usually more expensive) than a rectangular-cut bag. Rectangular-cut bags, with or without insulation, are usually fine for summer camping in the flatlands. But when overnighting outdoors in cool or cold weather, buy a bag with plenty of insulation.

My personal preference when car camping is a generous-cut rectangular bag containing 6 pounds or more of insulation. Such bags are heavy and bulky, but I like the freedom of movement and the wonderful feel of weight—they remind me of a New England comforter—over my body.

Lighter mummy or modified-mummy bags are the choice of backpackers heading for high country. They warm more quickly because they trap air better. But they are also confining, so much so that some campers report mild attacks of claustrophobia.

When manufacturers make sleeping bags, they must sew through the insulation to hold it in place between inner and outer liners. Otherwise, the insulation will shift and ball up. The stitching process, however, pinches the insulation along the seam and results in less loft. Summer-weight bags usually include a single layer of insulation, quilted to the inner and outer liners. Better-quality bags feature more insulation, which has to be layered—usually in an innovative shingle or overlapping quilt design—to avoid pinch points. Down bags typically are constructed with slant baffles for this same reason.

All bags take on moisture from respiration and perspiration by the sleeper. More expensive bags are treated for water repellency and some newer top-of-the-line bags may contain DryLoft, a new Gore membrane that stops wind, is breathable and—by itself—is waterproof (unless the seams are completely sealed, no bag is truly waterproof). Liners are typically nylon, too, because the material aids drying by air and sun the next morning. Although they feel wonderful next to your body, cotton flannel liners suck up moisture and can be hard to dry out.

Other signs of construction quality are full-length left- and right-hand No. 7 or No. 8 zippers that self-heal, insulated draft tubes over the zippers to keep cold air out, and roomy, insulated foot warmers. Zippered utility pockets on the outside are handy for holding change, eyeglasses and other small items.

The premier goose down bag from The North Face features DryLoft, a new breathable, windproof membrane from the W. L. Gore Company.

Bags for Extreme Cold

Avid campers and backpackers always own more than one sleeping bag to give them options when weight, bulk and optimum warmth are considerations. I have spent enough miserable nights shivering outdoors to overly compensate for warmth (remember the old saying: "You can always take it off if you're too warm."), and so I usually pack a warmer bag than I think I'll need.

You never know when a dependable cold-weather sleeping bag will come in handy. An injured person can survive several days in one, and they are an excellent hedge against hypothermia, the nation's number one killer of outdoor enthusiasts.

To my mind, fine goose down is as good as it gets for insulation. Be advised, however, that some products labeled as containing "down" can include as much as 20 percent feathers, according to Federal Trade Commission standards (if you want pure down, check the label for

"100 percent down"). And pay attention to a term called "fill power," which refers to down's ability to loft. The lightest, finest goose down (650- to 700-fill) fluffs best.

As with underwear, you can't test a new sleeping bag, then take it back to the store if you don't like it. So shop wisely. Among the hundreds of sleeping bag models now available, here are a few excellent cold-weather bags (zero degrees F. or below) containing copious amounts of goose down to consider: Slumberjack Down Range, North Face Solar Flare DL and Western Mountaineering Bristlecone.

Excellent synthetic choices include Coleman Elk Hunter II and Woods Canada Marksman 8 (containing six and eight pounds respectively of Hollofil II), L.L. Bean Outdoorsman (Quallofil), Moonstone Mountaineering Maxima (PolarGuard), VauDe Arctic II and Sierra Designs (both with Micro-loft) and Caribou Winter (PrimaLoft).

CAMPING AND BACKPACKING STOVES

A few years ago a fascinating little book called *Roughing It Easy* by Dian Thomas became a national bestseller. In it, the author described clever ways to make camp stoves from tin cans, a reflector oven from a cardboard box lined with tinfoil, even a Dutch oven from an empty can slid inside another. Over the years I have tried some of these make-your-own camp stoves, and they worked. But it would have been far easier to pack a clean-burning, fuel-efficient commercial camp stove. Then I wouldn't have had to gather dry wood and build a fire.

Wood fires, assuming they are even allowed in the places you camp, are going the way of Sterno. Remember Sterno, the heat in a can, made from a jellylike substance rich in alcohol? Restaurants still use Sterno

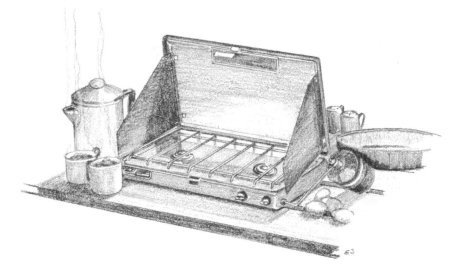

Modern camp stoves have come a long way since the smoking kerosene burners of an earlier generation. Light in weight and efficient, many new stoves burn a wide range of fuels.

for keeping buffet dishes hot, but few campers rely on Sterno anymore. Nor do they build wood fires for cooking. Campfires may be great for toasting marshmallows and sharing stories, but who wants to dodge sparks and inhale smoke while sweltering over a wood fire? And who is going to scrub clean those blackened pots and pans?

Fuel Considerations

The biggest choice today's campers face is whether to buy a modern camp stove that runs on *propane, butane* or *liquid camping fuel.* All are good but there are differences in cost and convenience. Relying on bottled propane eliminates the need to pour or pump liquid fuel because the pressure in a propane cylinder is constantly regulated, although you may have to make periodic adjustments. Propane is more expensive than liquid camping fuel, though, and because there is no way to be sure when you will run out, it is wise to pack an extra cylinder or two.

On the other hand, if you plan to set up camp for a few days, you might want to invest in a refillable, 5-pound, 10-pound or larger bulk propane

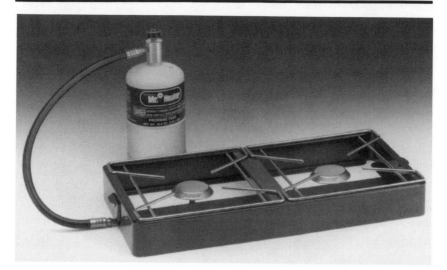

Clean-burning, non-spillable propane is the most popular of fuel choices among many campers.

container. Besides spending less than half as much for the same amount of fuel, you will eliminate having to dispose of the smaller empty cylinders.

Like propane, butane is a liquified gas which is used as a fuel in some foreign-built camp stoves, usually small backpacker models. But in recent years butane has fallen in popularity overseas, too, as more and more campers turn to propane. One of butane's biggest disadvantages is that it comes in seven-ounce non-resealable cylinders which are not puncture-proof. On an Alaskan trip a few years ago, my partner and I had to leave his butane-fired stove and fuel containers at the airport in storage because airline officials would not approve their going aboard. Another disadvantage of butane is that it has lower BTU output than other fuels. And it handles poorly in wind.

As with butane, pressure in a propane tank drops rapidly as temperatures slide; in cold weather, frost will actually form on the cylinder as it releases fuel. At 70 degrees, pressure will be 110 pounds per square inch (psi). But when the temperature drops to 50 degrees, the pressure falls off to 77 psi. At 30 degrees it is only 55 psi, and at zero only about 20 percent of the original pressure remains. To perform well, propane requires steady release of pressure. When pressure diminishes, heat output eventually falls off.

Although light in weight and therefore popular with backpackers, butane fuel cartridges can't be recycled.

Propane has been available for household use for about ninety years and is more easily found today than ever before. Even so, liquid camping fuel is even easier to obtain. That which is commercially prepared and sold in two-gallon cans is basically naptha, an odorless, colorless raw material for gasoline that is often used as a solvent and cleaning fluid. Naptha began to replace kerosene, which was oily and smelly, about thirty years ago. Available from sporting goods stores and outfitters, the super-refined liquid camping fuel burns cleanly and efficiently and is less expensive than propane.

Unleaded gasoline can be used in a pinch in camp stoves and other appliances requiring liquid fuel, but prolonged use will shorten the appliance's life and reduce its performance. Although cleaner than leaded gas, unleaded fuel contains more additives and impurities than does liquid camping fuel.

The Coleman Company recently introduced a line of stoves that run on unleaded gasoline as well as liquid camping fuel. When camp stoves malfunction, nine of ten times the problem is a dirty or otherwise faulty generator. So company engineers designed a generator that reduces clogging while it increases vaporization. A big advantage of unleaded gasoline is its worldwide availability. In an emergency, a camper could siphon some from his vehicle fuel tank. It is also the cheapest of all camp stove fuels.

So, should you use propane or liquid camp fuel or unleaded gas?

Coleman engineers have redesigned the generators on certain products to burn unleaded gasoline as well as liquid camping fuel.

Relative costs may help you decide. Unleaded gasoline is four times less expensive than liquid camping fuel and up to twenty times less costly than propane. Backpackers and campers who want to travel light should consider a one-burner stove. New ones weigh a little more than a pound empty and less than two pounds full. They hold more than two hours of unleaded gas or liquid camping fuel and fit into a coat pocket or tuck into a backpack cranny.

These state-of-the-art stoves operate in subfreezing temperatures and don't require preheating or priming. On the other hand, they flare up more often than propane or butane. For this reason, don't use them to heat your tent and never cook inside your tent.

Larger one-burner stoves that run on bulk propane come equipped with cooking pot and cover and are designed for fish boils and other communal cooking projects. These big stoves are also ideal for family picnics and backyard barbecues, helping campers to stretch their investment.

For serious family or group camping, however, you'll want to step up to a two-burner or three-burner stove, either propane or liquid fuel-fired. A double-burner typically weighs about 12 pounds. Some models feature separate propane cylinders, and we have found these to be more efficient. Why? Because with single cylinder units, the secondary flame pot is never as steady nor as strong as the first, which is closer to the fuel source. Three-burner stoves available today operate at peak output of more than 20,000 Btu's. Prices are generally under $100, and with proper use and care, the stove will last a lifetime.

You can't make a mistake by choosing either type of camp stove. Propane units are the simplest of all to operate because the shutoff valve is about the only part that can wear out. Although liquid fuel appliances require a generator, new models are self-cleaning. Some types even feature electronic ignition.

New, innovative stoves are coming onto the market all the time. The Sierra Stove, which puts out up to 18,000 Btu's per hour when fueled with wood, charcoal or other fuel, will boil a quarter of water in four minutes and is not affected by altitude. That feature—plus its 15-ounce weight—makes the stove, manufactured by ZZ Corporation, perfect for campers and backpackers. Options include a wrap-around windscreen, liter pot and grill.

Wood-Burning Stoves

No wall tent is complete without a wood-burning stove with a flat top for heating water and cooking. Traveling to various hunting camps throughout the years, I have seen stoves made from sheet metal and steel barrels cut in two. The smaller sheepherder types are handy for heating icefishing shacks in winter, too.

Commercial wood burners often feature a warming tray and water closet to provide hot water on demand. The more innovative designs, such as those available from Riley Stove Co. and Kozy Kamp, are light in weight (under 10 pounds) and collapse for easy packing of pipe and sidewalls in canoe or horse pannier.

Grills and Ovens

Backyard barbecue grills are fine for camping if you have the room to haul them. If not, bring the steel grate from the grill and balance it over a circle of rocks four to eight inches high to make your own barbecue pit.

Electronic-ignition appliances, such as this new Dual Fuel Power-house 414 two-burner campstove from Coleman, preclude the need for matches.

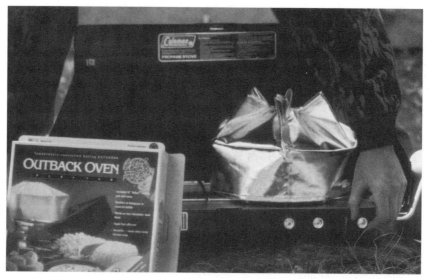

The author used his Coleman campstove and Outback Oven by Traveling Light to make pizza and brownies.

Sites in many commercial and public campgrounds feature stand-up grills or fire rings where all you have to do is bring the charcoal.

Some companies make collapsible grills that pack flat. Others produce lightweight reflector ovens that either fit over a burner plate, such as the Outfitter Oven by Fox Hill Corporation and the Outback Oven by Traveling Light, or accept charcoal. The little ovens work well for preparing bread, cobblers, casseroles and other baked delicacies.

LIGHT, HEAT AND POWER SOURCES

Fire is a camper's best friend, but after the flames die, the need for a source of artificial light and sometimes heat becomes important. If the campground has electricity, the problem is easily solved by bringing a mechanic's light on a long cord and a small heater to warm your tent. You can even make your own electricity with a portable, gas-powered generator.

Lanterns

As a boy I owned an old green Coleman lantern that went everywhere that boys go to find adventure. It provided heat and light and held back night's dangers as we camped in pup tents throughout the neighborhood. The lantern tagged along on my first Great Lakes smelt dipping excursion. We used it regularly for nightcrawler hunting expeditions when we needed fishing bait. The lantern's soft glow wouldn't spook the biggest crawlers that stretched over a mown lawn like wet rubber bands. Always the lantern was more practical and cheaper than burning up D size batteries in our official Boy Scout flashlights of army green.

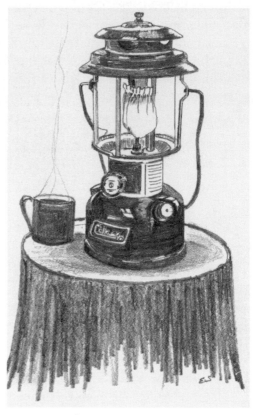

The Coleman Company has made more than 45 million lanterns since William C. Coleman built the first one in 1914.

Who knows what happened to that old dependable Coleman lantern? It probably ended up in one of my parents' garage sales, or maybe Dad swapped it for a fishing reel. Perhaps some kid is using it yet today. Why not? Lanterns older than that one are still on the job and going strong.

Since founder William C. Coleman's invention of the "arc lantern" in 1914, the company has sold about *45 million* lanterns around the world. Coleman lamps have safely guided rural surgeons' hands and lost sailors to shore and have been standard gear among camping explorers from Africa to Antarctica through much of the twentieth century. Many of the stories involving their use are legendary, like the Coleman lamp that was used as a signal in Mesa Verde National Park in Colorado. Forty miles away a rancher thought he had found a new star.

The arc lantern became a boon for campers and is one reason the sport grew so rapidly between the two world wars.

I grew up near Flint, Michigan, and was eight years old when a killer tornado struck in 1953. The Coleman Company has always loaned emergency lanterns to communities facing natural disasters. They shipped 200 to Flint; for some reason, 202 were returned.

There is a certain reassurance to the hiss and sputter of a burning lantern, and I can't imagine camping without having one throw its warm and welcome yellow light over my tent. Fuel-burning lanterns are a safe, clean, convenient, economical and durable source of light.

Modern campers have a smorgasbord of good products to choose from, including all the fuel and lighting options discussed under stoves.

Coleman Gold Top mantles have all but eliminated one complaint of campers—how to keep a mantle from breaking.

In addition, we now have battery-run fluorescent lanterns that recharge with home or campground electricity, in a car's cigarette lighter, or by the sun. Lanterns have grown so small in size and light in weight that some backpackers prefer them over flashlights. At least one company makes a remote-controlled lantern. You can hang it halfway to the public restroom and turn it on or off from your tent. Other models attach to the same propane tank that fuels a camp stove.

Most lanterns get their source of light from a mantle or mantles that have been properly burned off to a fine ash. Since their invention in 1885 mantles haven't changed their looks much, but today's products are much stronger and last longer. Coleman Gold Tops, for example, are constructed of a fine rayon yarn containing yttrium, a rare-earth mineral used to improve red spectrums in color TV screens. Gold Tops have proven to be four times stronger than their predecessors. Occasionally, though, any

Lanterns require little maintenance. Wrapping the globe with a foam rubber protector is a good idea to prevent breakage in transit.

mantle may need replacing, and cracked glass globes and the occasional gummed generator are other problems to expect.

Other Sources of Light

Other lighting sources available to campers include powerful spotlights that plug into vehicle cigarette lighters, sealed beam flashlights and headlamps, and generator-produced electricity.

Always pack at least one flashlight along with spare batteries. The newer personal "mini" lights that rely on AA or AAA batteries are ideal for backpacking. Better ones are made from aircraft-grade anodized aluminum and feature adjustable spot-to-flood beams. The head may be removed on some models so they can double as an area light to illuminate a small tent.

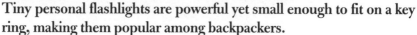

Tiny personal flashlights are powerful yet small enough to fit on a key ring, making them popular among backpackers.

Standard color on most minis is black. Tip: Buy one in a bright color or with an optional belt holster, or attach it to your car key ring so you won't lose it. Investing in a waterproof model is also a good idea. Brinkmann Legend minis are available with interchangeable lenses of red (improves night vision and won't disturb your sleeping partner), amber (cuts through fog and smoke), and blue (shines through glass).

Two tiny personal lights with red LED beams are make by Tekna, a division of Rayovac. The Private Eye is smaller than a car key to which it attaches. The Card Lite is the size of a credit card and weighs less than an ounce. The company also makes the Mono-Lith, a keyring light powered by a lithium battery that may last for years.

A small headlamp comes in handy for camping, too, because it frees up the hands. Streamlight Topspot II is a convertible flashlight/ head-lamp with adjustable focus and 45 degree tilting head. It operates on four AA batteries. Liston Concepts makes a headband called the Jak-strap which uses Velcro to hold a mini flashlight at several angles.

Candles are an excellent source of low-cost and emergency light (as

Campers appreciate being able to use both hands. The Jakstrap from Liston Concepts holds a mini light at several angles.

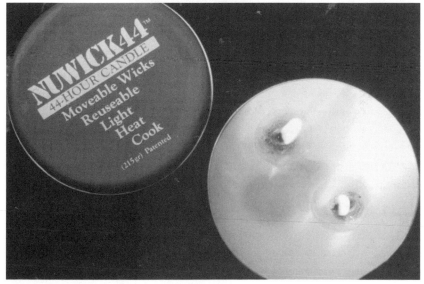

Backpackers also approve of the Nuwick 44-Hour Candle because it serves many functions and is light.

well as heat for warmth and cooking) and should find their way onto every camper's and backpacker's checklist. Nuwick, Inc. produces a candle in a can with removable floating wicks that burn for 40 hours or more.

Heaters

Stoves and lanterns afford summer campers all the tent heat they'll need. But at other times of year—and especially in mountain country—a source of radiant heat can make the difference between misery and comfort. A number of small, portable heaters, powered either by electricity or fossil fuels, give today's campers plenty of opportunities.

Whenever I'm tent camping by car and the temperature threatens to fall below 30 degrees, I pack a small propane-fired heater that shuts on or off with the flip of a switch. I use it only for a few minutes each morn-

Mr. Heater propane radiant heater can remove the chill from four-season campers.

ing before changing sleepwear for warmer clothing, and I'm careful to open a window for ventilation.

Wall tents with small wood-burning stoves ventilated via pipe through the roof can be uniformly heated and kept warm around the clock. Coming in from hunting or hiking all day in bad weather, you will appreciate the toasty warmth. The stoves are perfect for drying wet footwear and clothing, too.

Generators

A portable generator is a great way of adding heat and light to camp and of juicing small appliances and hand tools. Direct current (DC) outlets allow you to charge a battery on your flashlight, car, boat or electric

This Honda portable generator ran quiet and was fuel efficient in the author's Michigan bird-hunting camp.

trolling motor. The quiet-running, fuel-efficient generator requires little maintenance and can be a life-saver in home emergencies when the commercial power goes out. So if you're thinking of getting one for camping, consider buying a unit with enough power to drive a furnace fan (about 1,200 watts for a $1/3$ hp motor), air conditioner or refrigerator/freezer (about 2,500 watts for a 10,000 Btu appliance).

How much power do you need for camping? Simply match the generator's watt output to the watt demands you'll be making on it. If all you need is electric lights, for example, a 1,000-watt generator should be able to light 10 100-watt bulbs. A tiny 500-watt generator will power a window fan, microwave or small television although it won't run them all at once. Generally, you can add up the watts required, although in the case of appliances run by electric motors, you'll be closer to actual demands if you multiply by three. In other words, a 1,500-watt generator will steadily power (no surges) a 500-watt motor.

Check the manufacturers' specifications on the appliances you wish to run and then triple the watt demands to be sure. If demands are explained as amps, however, remember that amps times volts equals watts. For example, an appliance that draws eight amps will need 960 watts of juice (8 amps $\times$ 120 volts = 960 watts).

Standard. state-of-the-art features on most portable generators include noise suppressors, electronic ignition, spark arrestor, circuit breakers, pair of 120 volt plug-ins for alternating current (AC) and one 12 volt DC output. Some models have fuel gauges, frequency meters, automatic voltage regulators, oil level warning lights, and extra-large fuel tanks for longer running between fillups.

Because of their bulk, weight and fuel demands, generators are impractical for campers who move by muscle power. Some bristle at generators' intrusions into wilderness settings where any mechanical gadget that makes noise is not welcome. When appropriate, though, the generator serves a wonderful purpose for campers who like to smooth their experience.

PACKS

Anyone who has ever loaded a pack and headed over the mountain wonders (1) Do I have everything I need for this trip? (2) Could I have left anything behind to conserve space and lighten the load?

On a recent day hike with my wife in Montana, we chanced upon an experienced backpacker heading into the wilderness for two weeks.

The internal-frame pack fits the body's contour better than an external-frame pack and is better for hiking rugged terrain.

While chatting with us, he didn't bother to remove the 75-pound mega pack that towered over his head. "I do this every summer," he explained while leaning on a walking stick. "I like to get in back of beyond, but it takes a lot of planning. Kitchen, bedroom, bathroom—it's all in this pack, all thought out beforehand."

This backpacker in Montana's Glacier National Park was toting 75 pounds in his Mountainsmith pack.

Daypacks

I considered the contents of my wife's and my shared daypack: mini fishing reel and collapsible rod, fruit and trail mix, binoculars, ponchos, water filter, pocket camera, bird and flower identification guides, a slim paperback. Although the load weighed only a dozen pounds or so, everything we needed for the day's outing was there.

Our pack is big enough to carry a one-man tent and other overnight gear, and it features lash tabs for securing a sleeping pad and bag. I bought the pack with such multiple outdoor uses in mind; on other ventures, it has held deer hunting or fishing paraphernalia.

Unless you're purely a backpacker, such crossover consideration is important when buying a pack. It can also help you to choose the type of pack best suited for your purpose. Because dozens of manufacturers have flooded the market with packs of all sizes, shapes and colors, sort-

The author loves his Duluth Pack rucksack for canoe camping.

ing through the maze to find value and quality is a formidable chore. Begin by eliminating what you don't want or need.

Rucksacks

Rucksacks in one form or other have been around since the days of the voyageurs, and companies like Duluth Tent & Awning and Granite Gear still make the frameless workhorse packs in canvas or Cordura. Designed to fit needed space such as the bow of a canoe, a balanced pair slung over the pommel make ideal panniers on a pack animal. With the aid of a tumpline I've used these original backpacks for traditional purposes, like hauling trapped beavers and quartered elk. A 50-year-old relic rucksack I saw in Alaska was still in service. When the shoulder straps wore out, the owner, who is an outfitter and guide, simply roped it to a packboard.

External-Frame Packs

External-frame packs are fine for walking off magnum loads in open terrain for short distances. The key is to position as much of the load as

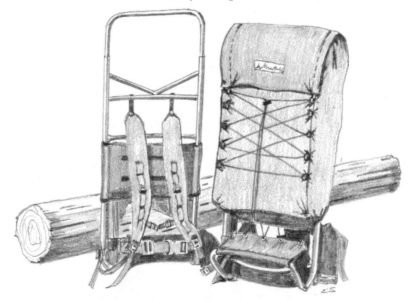

Some external-frame packs can be used as packboards when the pack material is removed.

possible over the body's natural center of gravity and let the pack's outer frame distribute weight to the hip and pelvic area with the aid of a padded hip belt. Look for this feature as well as quality in the frame itself. V-truss frames should be heli-arc welded, not soldered, and there should be cross bars and vertical struts for stability.

Tip: Always carry a couple of extra clevis pins and split rings in case of breakage. The external-frame pack is all but worthless if it separates from the frame and can't be repaired on the spot.

Internal-Frame Packs

Internal-frame packs are the better choice when balance is important, such as negotiating a talus or crossing a river. Designed to hug the body's shape, these tapered, well-padded packs can be individually form-fitted—

Side load compressors on this Remington internal-frame pack by Nelson / Weather-Rite help the hiker to fit the pack to his body.

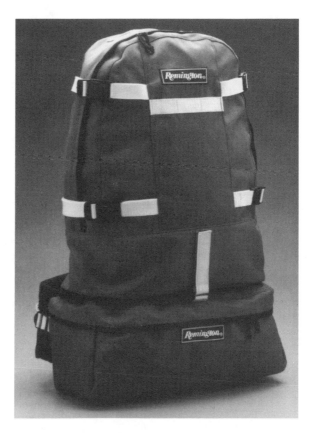

like shoes and suits—and are less bulky and more responsive than external-frame packs. Adjustable sternum, hip, shoulder and side stabilizing straps and removable back stays help to lock down a load.

Much has happened since Richard Kelty designed the first aluminum backpack frame in his garage shortly after WW II. Understanding the nature of computer-designed backpacks made from high-tech materials—the names of which are often unpronounceable—can be intimidating to a newcomer. Advice: Break into the sport slowly through day hiking, then slowly increase your stamina and weight loads to accommodate overnight trips. Consider renting a backpack and other gear before buying anything.

Know that most packs are made from polyurethane-coated nylon, which means they are water repellent, not waterproof. Even a membrane must have its seams sealed in order to block water effectively. If in doubt, buy a waterproof rain cover or pack a garbage bag.

Packs should fit the wearer's body like a suit of clothes. A competent salesperson can show the way.

In the Northeast
the ash packbas-
ket is still popular
among traditional
backpackers.

Getting Fit

When it comes time to choose equipment, ignore the high-tech hype and go simply for fit. Fit begins with the right pack size for your torso length.

Some companies measure torso from top of shoulder to hip bones. Others, more technical, tape from the neck crease with the head tilted back to the illiac crest (two inches below the top of the hipbones). A competent salesperson can help, especially with sizing for harness and hipbelt and making sure you actually know how to adjust a loaded pack.

According to the makers of Osprey packs, there are eight impor-tant, chronological steps to the adjustment process as applied to their models. But every pack maker is different. For instance, another com-pany, Vortex, has designed an air bladder system with built-in hand pumps to help adjust fit to load. With any pack, do it improperly, and you'll be rubbing ointment on chafed body parts at night. That's why it's a good idea to walk around the store's parking lot for an hour, then ask the sales clerk to assist in any final adjustments before forking over your credit card.

Pack Options

Some of the better-built magnum packs can be broken down into smaller carryalls for light duty such as day tripping, hunting and fishing. Know, too, there is a growing number of lightweight specialty packs. Johnson Camping's Camp Trails Wilderness Pack comes with a handy "kitchen sink" organizer pocket. Lone Peak makes bicycling packs as well as chest and fanny packs for fishing. Fenwick's new backpack for fishermen has rod tube sleeves and adjustable compartments for tackle.

COOLERS

Researchers studying unearthed remains of a mastodon killed in the Midwest more than 10,000 years ago found evidence that hunters had attempted to preserve the meat. Chunks of ice whacked from a nearby glacier probably helped cool the kill and keep it fresh. Then for several thousand years permafrost maintained the cache in a frozen state. The ancient Greeks preserved meat with creosote. Various North American Indian tribes dried fish and meat, making jerky and pemmican that lasted for months.

Hard-Plastic and Steel Coolers

Preventing food from spoiling is a challenge that all campers have faced, but today we can choose from a wide range of practical and high-tech coolers that take away the worry. Most are rigid-walled containers of hard plastic or steel and polyfoam (also called polystyrene foam) models that vary in thickness and density. Sizes range from 6-quart personal models to 178-quart bruisers designed for offshore fishing. Expect to pay $1 to $2 per quart for family camping sizes from 25- to 100-quart

A 40-quart cooler like this Rubbermaid model is the standard size for family camping.

capacity. The behemoth marine models can run $300 to $400.

The stylish softpack coolers, which are fine for tailgate parties, are impractical for camping because they are not crush-proof.

All hard-plastic coolers are insulated with foam. Those that are steel-belted or contain metal sidewalls are heavy but are virtually crush-proof and last a long time. Some companies build metal coolers for strength but then add a plastic lid to cut weight.

Hard-plastic coolers now come with ice and storage trays that convert to serving trays, dividers that can be used for cutting boards, and cushions that double as boat seats. Some even feature lids that function as secondary coolers and as reversible beverage holders. A few sport fish-measuring scales and lights built right into their plastic lids. These injection-molded, space-age coolers are light and rustproof, virtually unbreakable and support weights to 300 or more pounds. They resist stains and odors and are easy to keep clean.

Thermoelectric coolers

An old joke about coolers and beverage containers asks "How do they know when to keep things cold and when to keep them hot?" A few

Thermoelectric coolers, like this Coleman model, also become food warmers. Power sources include 12- and 110-volt systems.

years ago, the answer might have been propane. Today, it lies in the electrical plug, thanks to thermoelectric coolers being made by several companies. These nifty coolers plug into an automobile cigarette lighter or any other 12-volt power source. A special adaptor allows campers to tap into 110-volt systems at home or in the office. Reversing the plug changes the cooler to a portable food warmer with a fan that distributes heat evenly. The range with some models is about 40 degrees below zero to 70 degrees above ambient temperature. Retail price of a 36-quart model is from $150 to $200.

COOKWARE

Over the years cast-iron cookware remains the first choice of campers because it heats evenly over any kind of fuel source. Anyone who has enjoyed a shore lunch prepared by a Canadian guide in one of those 10-pound lumberjack skillets or who has eaten bean-hole beans made in a Dutch oven surely will agree.

Dutch Ovens

The Dutch oven is a cross between a heavy-duty frying pan and an old iron kettle. Some have three stubby legs and all contain a heavy flanged lid. Sizes vary from 8 to 16 inches in diameter and from 3 to 6 inches deep. They are as simple and useful to modern campers as they were to the pioneers and mountain men. It is said that Paul Revere himself perfected an early Dutch oven.

They can be used to cook literally anything—bread, biscuits, pies, cakes, cobblers, roasts, beans, soups, puddings, stews, steaks, chops and pancakes. The Dutch oven's weakness is its great weight and propensity to rust if not cared for properly. Cast iron is porous and if scrubbed hard with strong detergent will rust. After use I always clean my Dutch oven with a warm, wet cloth (never a scouring pad), then let it dry before wiping it with a little vegetable oil or shortening.

Aluminum Cookware

Aluminum cookware is lighter and usually less expensive, but a too-cheap set of pots and pans, cups and plates will scorch food, burn

The Dutch oven is an American tradition among campers who like to cook everything from beans to biscuits.

The author sorts through his collection of stainless steel cookware, which nestles together for easy toting in a spare cooler.

tongues and lose heat quickly. If you choose aluminum, buy the best-quality equipment you can afford; in particular, look for skillets with Teflon coating. Enamel steel and stainless steel cookware offer excellent compromises between cast iron and aluminum. Several companies

Melmac dishes
and retired home
kitchen cookware
serve extended
duty in camp.

make one- to six-person cooking kits of aluminum or steel where the
various-sized parts neatly telescope into each other and have folding
handles for tidy packing. Prices begin at $5 to $10 but can run to $50 or
more. Such cooking kits are a must for backpacking although most veterans buy items individually and assemble the kits themselves.

To save money, consider retiring home kitchen cookware that shows its
age to the camping gear box. A few years ago for $2.50 at a rummage sale
I picked up a complete set of Melmac dishes, which I still use for family
camping. If you buy a personal mess kit, choose heavy plastic because it is
lighter than most metals, cleans up easily, and retains heat longer. Glass is
out. A double-walled, stainless-steel mug is my favorite item because it's
unbreakable and won't burn my tongue, yet it keeps coffee hot. On long
hikes I'll substitute a lightweight cup of Lexan plastic.

Fine for picnics, paper plates are all but worthless for camping. Once
soiled, they don't burn easily and must be hauled out with other trash.

Specialty Cookware and Utensils

Specialty cookware in any camp with several people or one that lasts for
a week or more includes two or more 10-quart galvanized pails for heating water, a Teflon-coated aluminum griddle that spans two burners on

a cookstove, and a 4-quart steel coffeepot of baked-enamel. A long-handled barbecue set of tongs, spatula and fork come in handy, as does a spare pair of Vice-Grip pliers for lifting hot lids and kettles.

OTHER ESSENTIAL GEAR

Knives

Hardly a day goes by, whether I'm camping or not, that I don't use the small two-bladed penknife that can always be found in my pants pocket. Campers need a sharp blade for cutting rope, slicing food, cleaning fish, making a fuzz stick to use for fire kindling, and many other chores. Swiss Army Knives and their imitators are especially useful because they contain various other tools that campers often need—an awl for punching holes in torn canvas that needs sewing, a screwdriver for

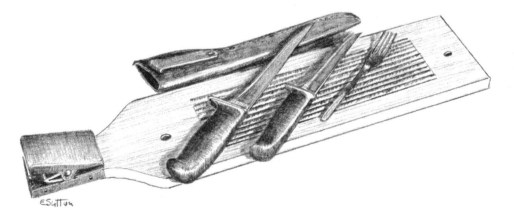

Specialty cutlery like these filleting and skinning knives serve a useful purpose for campers.

tightening a loose bail screw on a fishing reel. The corkscrew and openers for bottles and cans come in handy, too.

If you invest in such a knife—and I recommend you do— get a belt sheath for it. Better-quality knives usually come with such a case. So do the newer vari-purpose tools like the Leatherman and Gerber Multi-Plier Tool that are small enough to fit in the hand, yet strong enough to repair basic problems on a car engine. Campers never know when they'll have a need for pliers, a file, wire cutters or a phillips screwdriver.

Specialty edges like fillet knives, paring knives and carving knives, as well as stones or other devices for sharpening them, are additional wise choices for extended camping trips.

Hatches, Axes and Saws

At one time the ax was the single most important tool a camper could own. Legendary uses included cutting firewood, shaping poles for a tripod or lead-to shelter, pounding tent stakes, blazing a trail, and trim-

The much-maligned hatchet is still a good camp tool. Always wear gloves when chopping but never leave a hatchet or ax buried in a log.

ming pine boughs for a bed. I still pack a single-bit ax on long destination trips but opt for a hatchet (also called a belt ax) for shorter trips. When weight is a consideration, such as when backpacking, I carry my belt knife and leave the heavier hardware at home.

Smaller modern tents are self-erecting, precluding the need to chop tent stakes. Also, cutting live trees for any purpose is considered taboo in many campgrounds, both wilderness and suburban. Still, the ax and hatchet—even though many veterans shun the latter as dangerous and unnecessary—have their uses. Thanks to a hatchet, a hunting partner and I one time were able to open a tin of meat, the only container of food we had. Canoe campers always need to widen the portage trail in tight places. In a pinch, an ax or hatchet doubles as a hammer or shovel although such uses should be avoided whenever possible.

Double-bit models can be dangerous and are best left to skilled woodsmen. Choose a single-bit and, for the ultimate in safety, select an all-steel tool, one where the head and handle are forged. A rubber-coated handle cushions shock and aids in grip on these models. Hickory handles might cost less and look better but eventually the steel heads tend to loosen from the wooden handles. If you buy such a product, make sure wedges have not been added to fill space gaps. Better-made models bond wood to metal with chemicals.

The Pac-Saw from Natpro, Inc. features both a fine-toothed blade and a coarse edge, along with a blunted front tip for safety. The black webbing belt case for the 13$1/2$-inch saw comes with a knife-sheath front.

Many new lightweight saws, some of which fold and can be carried in a backpack, have found their way onto the market. Personal saws like the Sawvivor from Dawn Marketing and the Pac-Saw from Natpro are very durable and do a surprising amount of work in a short time.

Rope and Bungee Cords

Camp for a week and you will find a dozen uses for rope from making clotheslines to boat anchors to hanging food from a tree limb out of the reach of bears. Bungee cords double as lantern hangers and cooler locks and have a dozen other uses. Short of wire, nylon is the strongest rope material known, and it has three times the breaking-strength capacity of manila. Disadvantages, though, are that nylon can stretch up to 20 percent of its original length, and trying to undo tight knots made with it can be tough on the fingers.

I actually prefer rope from natural materials such as hemp, sisal, manila

This pocket water bag from Johnson Camping holds 2 1/2 gallons of water and yet weighs only 3 ounces and will tuck into a shirt pocket.

or cotton even though they are not as strong as nylon—or even Dacron or polypropylene for that matter. I know, too, that naturally made rope won't last as long. It can develop mildew or even rot away if it is not stored in a cool, dry place. Yet nothing smells and feels like real rope.

Bungee cords come in lengths from nine inches to three feet. Most have steel S-hooks at each end although some newer models feature plastic hooks and are made from cloth so as not to damage car roofs when used as tie-downs for canoes, bicycles and other gear.

Miscellaneous Gear

A small shovel is a handy item to have in camp. If space is a consideration, consider buying a folding model from an army/navy surplus store or a mail-order catalog.

You'll need something to carry and hold water. Some traditional campers still rely on heavy, 10-gallon steel milk cans, but they require two people to tote. More practical is the 5-gallon plastic jerry can with wide fill cap (or bring a funnel). Collapsible plastic containers are fine, too. A handy 3-ounce item I picked up recently for backpacking is the Pocket Water Bag from Camp Trails. The bag, which holds $2^1/2$ gallons of water without spilling, fits into a shirt pocket.

ITEMS FOR PERSONAL COMFORT

Simple pleasures like having a comfortable spot to sit and to place personal effects off the ground go a long way toward smoothing any camp. If you have room to pack it, a folding card table is especially appreciated. One of the handiest gadgets I have come across in recent

These durable hardwood camp chairs with comfortable fabric seats are made by Byer of Maine and come with their own carrying case.

Campers (below) appreciate folding portable tables like Coleman's Camp Kitchen, which contains shelving, a sink, work counters and even a chess board.

years is the Roll-A-Table, a clever 30-inch-square platform on four aluminum legs that rolls up into a six-inch-diameter bundle 30 inches long. I carry it in canoe and car trunk and even tossed it into a saddle bag once on a Western horsepacking expedition.

A lawn chair or folding camp stool with canvas seat is ideal when you want to change shoes, eat a meal or lounge around the campfire. If you have the time and talent, you can make camp furniture on site. Trim the branches from a dozen four-foot-long poles two inches in diameter, then lash the ends to tree trunks spread a few feet apart to make a temporary table. To fashion a clever chair, cut a straight section of log 36 inches long, then saw three-fourths of the way through the center and again from the top to the center. The chunk you remove will provide you with both a seat and a backrest.

Durable coolers double as camp seats. On a horsepacking trip to Montana, the head wrangler carried kitchen supplies in a pair of Rubbermaid refuse containers with flush-level lids. The big containers fit perfectly in panniers, then doubled as serving tables with boards placed across them.

Some companies make portable kitchens and sinks which make preparing food and cleaning up a snap.

Portable Shower, Toilet

The biggest complaint I hear from people who don't camp or who reluctantly participate is the concern of getting dirty and not being able to clean up in comfort. Companies have responded with no-rinse shampoos and with portable showers and toilets, the latter often used in RVs. A full-sized shower with privacy curtain called the Bivouac Buddy hangs from a tree limb and holds several gallons of warm water, which you pour in the top. Some backpackers, on the trail for several days, have taken to carrying lightweight portable solar showers made simply from a black plastic bag and a hose with shut-off clip. Three hours of direct sunlight will warm five gallons of water.

Clothing

Personal comfort means staying dry, warm and protected from the elements. When dressing for the outdoors, keep in mind your own defini-

Smart campers and backpackers are never far from rain gear and often carry a lightweight poncho or jacket on the trail.

tion of comfort—we are as different as our individual metabolisms—whether the planned activity is active or passive, and the kind of weather you expect to encounter. Then layer your clothing accordingly, and add or subtract according to changing conditions.

The inner layer formed by underwear, long underwear, T-shirts and socks lies next to the skin and allows perspiration to pass through to the secondary layer. Because polypropylene garments have a moisture regain of only .05 percent, they tend to wick moisture from the body and pass it to the secondary layer. The secondary layer—shirts, sweaters and pants, for example—absorbs this moisture while trying to keep you warm. The outer layer protects you from wind and rain. Raingear, insulated and non-insulated parkas and gaiters comprise this protective layer.

Heat always moves (radiates) from warm to cold, and in clothing either air or water helps move it along. It is important to stay as dry as possible because, according to tests by the W.L. Gore Company, water conducts heat away from the body 32 times faster than does air. Because cotton absorbs nearly 15 percent of its own weight in moisture, it dries slowly. At nearly double the moisture regain of 29 percent, wool dries even more slowly.

For summer camping activities that include berry picking, bird watching, day hiking, canoeing and bicycling, a pair of comfortable, wash-softened blue jeans and a long-sleeve flannel shirt (to protect you from the sun and biting insects) over cotton underwear will be comfortable. Add a baseball-style cap, cotton socks and tennies or lightweight walking shoes. A windbreaker or rain poncho often finds it ways into my fanny pack, along with sunglasses and sunscreen lotion of factor 20 or better.

A lightweight jacket or sweater helps ward off night's chill and those breezy passes in the high country. In spring and fall, I like to sleep in mid-weight polypropylene underwear and often wear it under a flannel or woolen shirt and trousers. But wool grows heavy when wet. Many campers and most backpackers opt for a lightweight outer jacket of Gore-Tex fabric.

Layering is most important when dressing for cold weather. The idea is to stay warm but not too warm because it takes energy to turn sweat into vapor and back again to a liquid—the phenomenon that occurs when the body overheats. Even a body at rest loses about a pint of water every 24 hours, mostly through respiration. So peel a layer the minute you begin to overheat, and don a layer as soon as you begin to get cold.

A Vapor Barrier Liner (VBL) over a thin sock or other next-to-the-skin layer will stop the flow of moisture from the body. But you'll need to change the inner layer of clothing more often because it will retain body moisture.

Footwear

Your choice of camping footwear depends most on your needs. Will you be backpacking in mountain wilderness or lounging at poolside at a KOA? Also, keep in mind that there are four major materials for boots

One-fourth of a person's bones are found in the feet. Proper sizing and then breaking in of new footwear is essential before taking to the trail.

and shoes: leather, rubber, canvas and synthetic materials such as Gore-Tex and Cordura.

Rubber is the ideal choice for wet conditions, but because it doesn't breathe, feet pay a sweaty price. Feet contain nearly 4,000 sweat glands per square inch, compared to a little more than 600 on a person's back. Canvas, on the other hand, is the least expensive material, breathes easily and dries fast. However, it is not waterproof, does not hold up well, and is poorly suited for cold weather. Soles of rubber and sides of canvas or Cordura, a tough, abrasion-resistant fabric, are often a better choice.

Tennis shoes and Tevas, Birkenstocks or other sandals are fine for knocking around, but the most comfortable footwear I've yet worn for general camping is a pair of mocassin-style, all-leather Irish Setter Country Walkers with three eyelets (for easy-on and off) and a Vibram sole with fairly aggressive tread for hiking and light backpacking.

Leather, of course, is not permanently waterproof and must be treated periodically with either oil or silicone, depending upon whether the leather has been oil-tanned or dry-tanned. A better choice, at least for active campers and most backpackers, is a pair of Gore-Tex hiking boots. The perfect all-around model is six inches high, features a full-length tongue, and comes with six to eight eyelets—the top pair of which are hook-style for speed lacing. The boot should have a decent bite on the sole for tackling mountain scree and a trash guard around

This six-inch-high hiking boot with Gore-Tex features a Vibram sole and ankle trash guard and is a good all-around boot for general hiking and light backpacking.

the ankles for keeping out sticks and debris (or pack a pair of gaiters). A pair should weigh no more than three pounds.

Backpackers toting heavy loads through uneven terrain need heavier, more rigid footwear to better protect ankles and dig in to soft earth. For travel across talus and other rock, plenty of cushioning will be appreciated at day's end. Removable liners that can be dried at night are a necessity if you're slogging through wet country or hiking in snow conditions. Both leather and synthetic fabric boots are popular and do the job.

Whenever you buy footwear for outdoor use, get measured by a skilled fitter who uses the time-honored Brannock device, which determines both longitudinal arch (distance from ball of big toe to heel) and latitudinal or metatarsal arch (distance from ball to knuckle of little toe). You'll know you have the right-fitting footwear if the edge of the ball lines up perfectly with the widest part of the boot or shoe. You can easily measure this by pinching with your thumb to find the ball through the footwear.

Another, older trick—although not as reliable—is to kick your toes as deeply into the boot as possible, then see if you can slide two fingers in back above the heel.

Get measured at day's end when your feet are their maximum size, stand when measured, and wear the same clean sock or socks you'll don for the trail. One foot will likely be larger than the other; size for it.

Wear a thin polypropylene sock next to the skin. The sock will wick away moisture to the outer sock, which should be wool, acrylic or a blend of the two. Companies like Thorlo and Fox River are now making wonderful specialty socks for on-the-go sportsmen. Never wear cotton tube socks for active outdoor sports. Cotton attracts moisture and then retains it. Socks ball up to create blisters. Change socks every day; if hiking for miles, change at midday, too.

WHAT TO TAKE, WHAT TO LEAVE HOME

The wise camper operates from checklists built from experience. For your first time out, put down everything you think you'll need, then revise the list when you get home. Cross out what you had no use for, and add what you forgot. I scratch very few items from my master

Planning begins with a
good checklist.

checklists, which I have arranged for All Camping, Personal, General
Camping, Kitchen Needs and Backpacking. I also have lists for RV and
Car Camping, Backpacking, Fishing and Camping, and Hunting and
Camping. No, I don't take everything on the list each time, but every-
thing is there to be considered.

Even so, there will be times when you'll pack twice what you need,
and you'll probably experience days when you wish you had remembered other things. Regardless of the type of trip you are planning, here
are some key items to always pack:

All Camping Checklist

• Ear plugs because I'm a light sleeper. Even if I wasn't, I'd pack
them anyway because some campgrounds are just plain noisy.

• Prescription medicine for a bad back. Riding a horse or climbing in
rugged high country have been known to throw out my back.

The author and freelance writer Ron Spomer with all their gear before embarking on a six-week camping adventure to Alaska. It all fit into the Jeep Cherokee!

• Spare eyeglasses and an eyeglass repair kit with tiny screwdriver and screws because if I break or lose the pair I wear, I'm sunk.

• A pocket compass because I don't need to be in deep woods to get turned around.

• A sponge and whisk broom. These two simple items go a long way toward keeping camp clean.

• Paper and pencil for leaving notes for buddies and potential rescue teams under windshield wipers on my truck. Also, if I don't write it down, I can't remember it.

• Change of clothes and footwear because getting dirty and getting wet is the price campers all too often pay.

• Roll of duct tape for fixing anything from tears in a wall tent to a split radiator hose on a vehicle.

• Pillow because sleeping on rolled-up bluejeans is not the fun it used to be thirty years ago.

• Portable table (if space and weight permit it) to add a touch of civilization to any camp.

• Waterproof matches because fire has always been a camper's best friend.

• Water filter cup (or tablets) for ensuring potable drinking water.

• Raingear because if you don't bring it, the heavens will pour.

• Flashlight and fresh batteries.

• First aid kit containing simple, basic in-structions.

• Emergency food such as granola bars and trail mix

• Plastic tarp and garbage bags because they serve so many unexpected uses.

• 10-foot piece of nylon rope for the same reason.

• Biodegradable soap

• Bandana

General Camping Checklist

Tent, poles, stakes
  and ropes
Sleeping bag
Sleeping pad
Cot
Lantern
Stove
Fuel
Hammock
Pillow
Pack
Camp permit
  (if required)
Candles
Canteen or water bottles
Cooker and propane

Hand saw
Small table
Folding chairs
Masking tape
Washbasin
Soap, shampoo
  and towels
Mirror
TV snack trays
Thick rubber bands
Bungee cords
Rope (100 feet or more)
Shovel
Knife
Camera and film
Ax and/or hatchet
Splitting maul
Heater
10-quart pails

Sawhorses
Water cans
Extra cooler
Hot pads
  or asbestos gloves
Food
Waterproof matches
Fire starter
Reading material
Portable toilet
Toilet paper, chemicals
Portable shower
Tow chain
Repair kit(s) for tent,
  lantern, etc.
CB radio or shortwave
  radio
Generator
Chain saw and fuel

Personal Checklist

Belt knife or pocketknife
Binoculars
Clothing to match
　the weather
Footwear (2 pairs)
Insect repellent
Compass
Medical card
Emergency phone
　numbers
Health insurance card
Prescription medicine
Sewing kit
Sunglasses
Toiletries
Spare eyeglasses,
　repair kit
Extra cash
Maps
Playing cards

Backpackers often like to know how far they traveled, and this Silva pedometer by Johnson Camping will tell them.

**Backpacking
　Checklist**

Lightweight tent
Sleeping bag
Sleeping pad
Backpack
Plateware and utensils
Cooking kit
Stove and fuel
Waterproof matches
Pedometer
Lightweight repair kit
　for tent, pack
Shoe Goo

Rope
Basic fishing gear
Point and shoot camera
Penlight, batteries
Duct tape
Seam sealer
Space blanket
Water bottle
Water filter or
　purification tablets
Food
Knife
Compass
Sewing kit
First aid kit
Candles

Lightweight reading
　material
Notepad and pen
Toilet paper
Raingear
Layerable clothing
　for climate and altitude
Hiking boots
Whistle

Kitchen Needs Checklist

Can opener
Cooler(s)
Wooden spoons
Thermos bottle(s)

These boat campers on Idaho's Snake River were able to haul extra gear like a Coleman Camp Kitchen.

Kettles for hot water	Salt, pepper, other	Utensils
Cutting block	condiments	Eggbeater
Aluminum foil	Skillet(s)	Griddle
Dishwashing items	Reflector oven	Barbecue utensils
(pan, soap,	Dutch oven	(tongs, fork, spatula)
brushes, cloths,	Whisk	Coffeepot
towels)	Water jug(s)	Sandwich bags,
Muffin tin	Plateware	lunch sacks
Potholders	(cups, glasses, bowls)	Cellophane wrap

This day hiker wouldn't forgive himself had he failed to pack a pocket camera.

Plastic bowls with covers
Garbage bags
Bottle opener
Pie plates

RV and Car
Camping Checklist

Spare keys
Owner's manual
Maps
Winch or come-along
Jumper cables
Tow chain
Snow tires/chains
Spare fuses, bulbs,
   headlamp
Spare tire(s)
Driver's license
Insurance certificate
Hydraulic jack
Vehicle registration

Tool box
Electrician's tape
Extra oil, transmission
   fluid, anti-freeze
Spare gas can

Fishing and
Hunting Checklists

Needs vary widely with
climate and type of activity. Partial lists to consider
include:

Fishing

Rod(s)
Reel(s)
Extra line
Landing net
Lures (jigs, plugs,
   spoons, spinners,
   flies, etc.)

License
Swivels and snaps
Leaders
Hook sharpener
Fillet knife, sharpener
Waders
Wading staff
Vest
Baitbox
Minnow bucket

Hunting

Bow, arrows
Licenses and permits
Topographic maps
Skinning knife
Meat saw
Muslin fabric
Gun case
Cleaning kit
Game cart
Block and tackle

II

LEARNING THE TECHNIQUES

After nearly forty years of sleeping outdoors, I can be mildly intimidated by the well-run camp, the person who ties rope knots without flaw, the guy who understands spatial relationships so well he can erect a tent without directions. I mean I'm supposed to be the expert, here, so how come I seem to have so much to learn?

Camping is forever giving us new places to go, new gear to try out, new methods and ideas to consider. You aren't going to learn everything in one lifetime, nor are you supposed to. One reason is because the rules change. Twenty years ago, for example, who would have thought the "leave no trace" mantra of the minimum-impact camper would be a household word?

Another reason is the explosion of new gear. Twenty years ago, William L. Gore was still trying to figure out how to stretch Teflon so thin it could be incorporated into fabrics—today the company makes 190 membranes. Who would have thought that lanterns would be light enough to backpack, would ignite without matches, and burn ordinary, unleaded fuel? Who could have imagined that technology would give us a hand-held electronic compass based on something called GPS? Global Positioning System relies on defense satellites to monitor exact loca-

71

An argument could be made that the maker of morning coffee has the most important job in camp.

tion, altitude and speed whether we're walking, riding a bicycle, driving a car or running a boat.

Computer software now allows us to make reservations at camp-grounds, find out which ones have wheelchair access, and what the weather is like in Australia for our planned Outback expedition. The world is more accessible than ever, modern technology gets us there quickly, and high-tech gear helps us adapt to the experience. An excit-ing world of camping awaits those of us with a streak of adventure.

Not everyone wants adventure, of course. Camping will always be an alternative to the blinking cursor and a world of call-waiting and four-lane frenzy. The goal of many campers is to relax, recreate, get to know their family, and maybe enjoy a taste of the natural world. However you camp, wherever you go,and why you do it, there are many things to learn. Important things like how to read a compass. Practical things like how to bring along a pet or get a good night's sleep. Simple things like how to change a lantern mantle.

Here for consideration are techniques and tips for smoothing your experience and making you want to return soon. You'll know the outing was successful when you sense a resigned reluctance to roll up the tent and pack the sleeping bags at the end of your trip.

PLANNING A CAMPING TRIP

I can't imagine taking any camping or backpacking trip without thinking through where I'm going and what I'll need. The sport demands that you plan carefully for comfort, necessity and emergency. Over the years, any time I've gotten lax in my organization, I've paid the price, like the time in Ontario when a friend and I ran out of food and matches and had to keep a fire burning while we waited three days for fog to lift so our bush pilot could freight us out. While clumsily transferring fuel from container to lantern, we experienced a minor explosion and nearly burned our shelter to the ground.

It's always something simple, like forgetting matches or a compass, that will foil the irresponsible camper.

On the other hand, the smooth-run camp, one that has been well-planned and is amply provisioned, is as comfortable as the best hotel. In one camp I'll never forget, our designated chef was a detail guy. He packed anchovies for the Caesar salad and tarragon for his special venison-with-shallots entree. Everything worked in that camp, including the backup stoves and lanterns.

Sure, a little luck and a lot of good weather are factors, too. But careful planning is the best way to realize your investment of time and money. Ignore planning and you may jinx your outing before tent stakes are out of the bag.

Sharing the Load

Unless you're a camping loner, you will have to rely on one or more partners to help with gear selection, chores and responsibilities. Pre-trip planning is crucial. Someone should hand out notepads to make individual and group check lists. Photocopy the lists so everyone knows what everyone else is bringing and what each person's responsibility is.

Focusing on a game plan, though, doesn't mean you can't change your mind when options arise. For instance, I never plan meals around catching fish or bagging game (I've gone hungry too many times), but if I happen to stringer a mess of stream trout, you can bet the pancake mix stays in the box for another morning.

The Five-Minute Camper

Ever find yourself trying to set up camp in the middle of the night under the glare of car headlights and curses of neighbors you've awakened?

While on their long camping trip to Alaska, the author and Ron Spomer shared the responsibilities of planning and preventive maintenance.

Good thing some-
one remembered
to pack the lantern
and propane fuel.

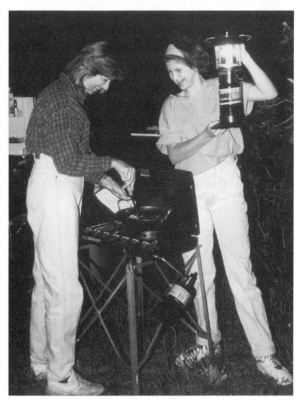

The five-minute camper is so organized that before the shut-off engine on his car has quit ticking, he can be in his tent, settling into a restful night's sleep. All it takes is a little planning.

Begin by choosing a lantern that ignites electronically—a flip of the switch and you have light. Practice setting up your tent so that it becomes second nature, or buy a self-erecting model like the Camel Six-tySecond Tent. While the tent is going up, open the air valve on your self-inflating mattress. Pull your sleeping bag from its stuff sack.

For the five-minute camper, it isn't a problem when the motels are all full or there isn't time to set up a detailed campsite. By chance or by choice, he'll be prepared by carrying basic equipment in the car and being able to set it up fast.

THE ART OF PACKING

S̲ome people are able to throw everything into a backpack and some-
how be able to zip shut the bulging contents. I'm a mule packer—I
fuss and fidget until I have a place for everything and everything in its
place. Space is always a problem, whether it's measured by the capacity
of pack, car trunk, folding camping trailer, canoe or saddlebag. As I
encouraged in the last chapter, a good checklist is the place to start.
Consider everything, then pack what you think you'll need—with an

This auto-camping couple in North Dakota was able to bring extra
gear as the result of careful selection and judicious packing in their
Chevy S-10 sport vehicle.

eye to space and weight. Faced with a half-mile-long portage, you'll regret having brought the 20-pound cooking griddle in your canoe.

Camping by Vehicle

Here are suggestions for camping by car or truck:

• Utilize the often-overlooked space under the car seats and the spare tire. A quality luggage rack will double space available. A small utility trailer will provide even more room.

• Use duffel bags for clothes because the bags assume their own shape. Give each member of the family a different colored bag.

• Make a fishing rod holder from four-inch PVC pipe, add caps to each end and attach to roof rack.

• Give children a plastic tub for storing souvenirs. Limit them to a single container (to put more in, something has to go).

The 3½-ounce PentaPure Travel Cup, will filter up to 3,000 cups of water and is ideal for backpacking.

• Use Tupperware-type containers. Not only are they waterproof, leakproof and stack neatly out of the way, when empty they double as wash basins.

• Maximize space and ease loading in the bed of your pickup truck or sport vehicle by laying 1 × 12-inch shelving boards across the wheel wells.

Loading a Pack

Using your checklist, lay out everything you need for your backpacking trip. Separate into two piles—one for daily convenience (sunglasses, camera, map, compass, trail snacks) and one for your destination camp (tent, sleeping bag and pad, cookware, utensils). Store nonessential stuff down and deep; keep convenience items handy.

Colored-coded stuff sacks (red for clothing, blue for food, etc.) help you to sort and store consistently. As a rule, internal-frame packs should carry most of their weight low. External-frame models can be loaded

Always load your pack in a consistent manner with gear items you might need along the trail in the easiest places to access.

Wranglers for Damnation Creek Outfitters in Montana use mantas to wrap fragile and loose gear before lashing to the horses.

more top-heavy. Side-to-side weight distribution is important in both styles. Terrain type also figures: In rough country, keep the center of gravity low; in even topography, the load can ride higher.

Lay the stuff sacks side by side in horizontal layers so as to conform better to the spinal curve. Internal-frame packs, which more easily conform to body shape, usually come with inside straps for compressing gear. For maximum comfort with either type pack, store hardware (stove, flashlight, cookware) to the outside rather than along your back. Side pockets are handy for convenience items. Lengthy items such as tent poles and fishing rods that don't easily fit inside should be lashed vertically to the pack.

The Science of Reduction

Think small and light, especially when the gear you bring will be toted on your shoulders:

• Wash clothes on the trail rather than pack extra changes. Polypropylene socks and underwear, for example, are very light in weight and can be washed and air-dried in minutes.

• Plan and prepare meals beforehand, bringing only what you need. Eliminate boxes, cans, jars etc. by carrying only the amounts needed in plastic bags.

• For example, put prepared meals into individual Zip-Loc bags (one meal per bag). The empty bags serve as refuse containers for packing out.

• Empty 35 mm film canisters are perfect for spices and other condiments. A tiny bottle of Tabasco, soy or Worchestershire sauce can put pizzazz into an otherwise bland meal.

• Pack extra candles instead of a heavy flashlight and batteries.

• Worms, grasshoppers, crickets, crayfish and other natural bait gathered at campsite often outproduce artificial fishing lures, which take up space and weight.

• Likewise, a telescoping rod and ultralight reel are good choices.

• The paperback novel you pack could be used to start a fire if necessary.

KEEPING DRY

There really is no excuse to get wet outdoors. Raingear is essential on all camping trips except perhaps desert outings. Here are other tips to consider:

• An overturned canoe makes an ideal temporary shelter for gear. In a lightning storm, though, stand under one of many evergreen trees close together (never a solitary tree, which could be a lightning target).

• Those Tupperware-type containers will keep dry your matches, towels and perishable foods.

• Dipping matches in paraffin will render them waterproof.

• A plastic garbage bag will double as a temporary rainsuit; simply cut holes for your head and arms.

• Make a simple, one-time dry sack from a heavy-duty garbage bag—

These Rubber-maid containers with tight-sealing lids keep food fresh and can keep other camping items dry.

This commercially made tarp gives campers shade and protects them from rain.

once filled, fold the top and seal with rubber cement.

• Invest in good raingear and a raincover for your backpack.

• A big piece of heavy-duty plastic takes up little space and comes in handy as an emergency tarp.

WHERE TO CAMP

A good campground is one that you can't wait to return to. The perfect location is the first step toward enjoying a quality, memorable experience. Nearly thirty years ago my young wife and I honeymooned for two weeks in a used 1962 Apache folding camping trailer. We were broke kids then, and we camped for free at the end of a forest road on Crown land in the wilds of Ontario. Our shelter was warm and dry, and we had the 17-mile-long lake to ourselves to canoe and fish. I don't remember if it rained; after all, we were in love.

Unfortunately, you can't go back to earlier times, and if you return to earlier places they may have changed, too. A little brook trout stream in northern Michigan where I used to camp and catch natives as long as a ruler has now been developed. Another remote campground where no one used to go is suddenly overrun with people.

Far from the Madding Crowd

Even though the nation boasts more than 16,000 public and private campgrounds, many of them are taxed to capacity. With one of every three or four Americans going camping these days, how do you find good places to go while avoiding the crowds? Some tips:

• Avoid the most popular parks and campgrounds during holiday

Ah, wilderness! Every camper's dream. During a recent year, an estimated 49 million people backpacked or camped in the nation's remaining wilderness.

weekends. Call ahead to (1) make a reservation, (2) find out what dates and time periods are poor ones to go.

• Camp during the off-season in spring and fall. You'll not only have your pick of choice sites but could also pay reduced rates.

• Camp near home. Some of the best campgrounds, many of them little-used, are within minutes of home. Municipal campgrounds run by local governments often are barely used all summer long.

• Target state and national forest campgrounds. They may be rustic and lack such facilities as running water, flush toilets and electricity, but those are also reasons why they rarely fill to capacity.

• Join a camping club. Membership may have its privileges, including reduced rates and preferred customer status at some camp-

This rustic state park campground in Michigan's Upper Peninsula was practically empty of campers in October.

grounds. For free lists of camping clubs and state campground associations, send a self-addressed, stamped envelope to R.V.I.A., Box 2999, Reston, VA 220900-999 .

• Apply for an off-site permit from the district forest ranger or local land manager. When available, the permits allow access to quiet areas away from the throng. Overnight camping is often permitted.

• In addition to camping opportunities on state land where you live (contact your state's park or recreation division), there may be large amounts of federal land with dozens of good campgrounds to consider.

Picking the Right Site

Few things can sabatoge your day of fun outdoors faster than waking up to a headache so bad your temples throb. Choose a level or slightly rolling tent site so that your head will be a bit higher than your feet. If you select a site with too much pitch, you'll end up looking like a beer pretzel at the bottom of your tent. Don't trust your eyes to find a level

The perfect campsite: morning sun, a few feet above river, away from insects and dead trees.

spot; stretch out on your opened sleeping bag and you'll soon know. I carry a small level when camping in a motorhome, travel trailer or pop-up unit to help me find the ideal spot to park for the night.

Choose an area for your tent that is reasonably open but not so isolated that it becomes a target for lightning or in such dense forest that dead limbs could come crashing down during a storm.

When camping along a river, watch out for rising water from storms or dam-floodgate releases. If pitching your tent along a slope, steer clear of gullies and beware of running water.

Search the site well for potential insect problems. Had I done that recently, I would have noticed several yellow jackets hovering mere inches above the ground. After my dog got stung, I had to move our tent. Grassy areas may be major breeding zones for biting insects. The site should be dry and far from stagnant water, a breeding ground for pesky mosquitoes.

Some wind may help keep insects away, but too much breeze can turn your sleep into a nightmare. So stay away from windward lake shores, and choose sites with an eastern or southern exposure if the prevailing winds are from the north or west. A point of partly forested land

During the heat of summer pitch your tent in an open area to take advantage of prevailing breezes.

jutting into a lake provides shade and some breeze. If possible, pitch your tent a few feet above the water—you could be ten degrees warmer.

Remember that cool air descends at night. In mountain country at a lowland site, this means that the evening/morning temperature difference can be 20 degrees or more, even in summer. Erecting your tent on the north or northeast side of trees provides afternoon shade. A west-side hill will allow morning sun and provide afternoon shade.

The perfect campsite isn't always a tree-encircled meadow nestled among the alpine peaks and lakes in a postcard setting. A few years ago a friend and I spent forty nights camping in Alaska and along the Alaska Highway. Each night, our favorite place to set up was in a roadside gravel pit. Why gravel pits? Because they were always level, quickly drainable, and in the open, far away from mosquitoes and black flies.

GETTING A GOOD NIGHT'S SLEEP

Having good gear and clothing and finding the right spot for your camp are the two most important keys to successful, hassle-free camping. They are essential to getting a good night's sleep, too, which is the basis for all outdoor fun lasting two days or more. Why? Because campers cranky from a rotten night's sleep make for bad bedfellows and

Camping begins in the backyard, always the best place to test new gear and check old gear for repairs.

surly neighbors. Tip: Set up on the campground fringe, away from main thoroughfares and restrooms. And take your time breaking in, turning beginning backyard experiences into overnighters close to home. As you gain experience, schedule in some weekend fun, then longer trips when you're ready.

When Nights Are Cold

Dampness and cold are the enemies that send many cold-weather campers searching for a motel. A little forethought and common sense will keep any sleeping bag dry. Such as, buy a quality bag with water-repellent, windproof shell. Or cocoon yourself by slipping the bag into a bivouac (bivy sack), which is waterproof. Other suggestions:

• Choose a sleeping bag with dark color to absorb the sun's warmth when you air dry it the next morning.

If your feet are cold, wear a warm hat. About half of a person's body heat is lost through his head.

• Change into dry clothes—preferably polypropylene underwear—before retiring for the night.

• Don't contribute to moisture problems by breathing into the bag.

• Zip open a window to ventilate your tent.

If you plan to spend several consecutive nights in subzero weather, add a Vapor Barrier Liner of nylon cloth, which you can purchase by the yard from a millinery or from camper supply outlets. The reason? Bags that don't get a chance to dry out in extremely cold weather collect body moisture in their insulation. This moisture freezes and can literally add pounds of ice to an untreated bag.

What to do if you don't own a top-of-the-line sleeping bag?

• Wear a ski cap to bed.

• Eat a good meal, especially one rich in protein, carbohydrates and fat.

• Drink lots of liquids (but no alcohol because it lowers body temperature) before retiring.

• Lay a closed-cell foam pad next to the ground; put another pad of softer foam atop the first mattress.

• If sleeping on a cot, place a barrier (mattress, blanket, piece of carpeting) between it and your sleeping bag.

When Nights Are Hot

Rain, wind and cold weather are well-known tricks that nature uses to wreck campers' plans. But what about excessive heat? When the temperature and relative humidity each creep above ninety degrees, campers get crabby, partly because they don't think they can do much about it. For relief, they flock to the public showers at the state park campground or take another dip in the lake. Some start looking for an air-conditioned motel. A few head for home. Here are suggestions for staying put and beating the heat:

• Choose a big tent and, because heat rises, make sure it has plenty of head clearance.

• Select a tent with plenty of zippered windows to get cross-ventilation. Be sure to remove the rainfly, if so equipped.

• Sleep on a cot instead of a ground mattress so that cool air—that which is close to the ground—will circulate underneath you.

• Wear cotton underwear and sleep atop your lightweight sleeping bag. Fold a flannel sheet inside the bag. Even on the muggiest nights there is often some hint of breeze; when the welcome relief finally comes, open the sheet and crawl between its layers.

• Change sweat-soaked clothing daily and dry sleepwear and sheets in the sun each day. Air out your bag, too.

Although I nearly always recommend tents with sewn-in floors, there are exceptions. If there are no biting insects and no threat of rain, for example, a floorless tent can sometimes have its sides lifted a few inches to allow more air to circulate over sleepers. A simple lean-to shelter is less confining than a tent, too. Sleeping under the stars on a cot or in a hammock is another possibility.

I always pack insect repellent but rarely use it in hot weather. Who wants to add more sticky substances to his skin every few hours or breathe noxious citronella candle fumes in addition to hot air, especially when fine-mesh mosquito netting will keep flying pests away? Low-lying areas may be moist and cool, but they put you at risk from insect attacks. So, instead of pitching your tent on a river sandbar, keep to higher ground, preferably in an open area swept by the wind. The windward side of a lake will be cooler than the lee side, of course, and the higher

These backpackers slept cool by pitching their tent on an island bluff and removing the rainfly.

location—if 15 feet or so above the water—will be above the dew line.

I nearly always point my tent opening downwind, but during extreme periods of heat, it makes sense to aim the doorway into the face of prevailing breezes. Just be sure to stake down or anchor the tent securely because it can turn into a billowing parachute with little warning. Position the tent away from large boulders, which may retain the day's heat for hours after sundown. Pick shady spots with care; as mentioned, sole trees or those containing dead branches are potential widow-makers.

KEEPING FOOD FRESH

Options abound for keeping food fresh in camp. Years ago before the days of refrigeration and dry ice, campers employed simple, practical methods, which still work when the ice is gone or is otherwise unavailable. A wooden produce crate, wire or plastic milk container carrier is ideal for holding cans and bottles in stream current or lake shade. A burlap sack will also work.

Store eggs, butter and other perishables in empty glass mayo jars and put them in the container, too. If you're camping on a lake, the headwaters are generally the coolest spots, but you might keep an eye open for underwater springs, too. Weight the container with rocks if needed to get it to bottom.

You can air cool perishables in the shade by placing the food in a bag of cheesecloth or other material, such as muslin, which has been perforated to allow air to flow.

A cool, shady spot beneath low-growing ferns is a good place to dig a cellar for storing perishables. Because coolness results from the evaporation process, soak a towel or burlap sack two or three times daily and

Limiting your trips to the cooler and eating perishable items first are two ways to keep food cooler longer in camp.

cover the hole with it. Another tip is to stretch a piece of canvas or burlap over the hole and rig a water pail or can of water on a stick or branch above it. Punching a tiny hole in the can will allow water to drip slowly. If that trick seems too bothersome, then place one end of the cloth cover in a pan of water and absorption will do the rest.

Common sense can help keep food cool on extended camping trips. Since heat rises, for example, try to store ice above food rather than below it. That is why many of the new hard plastic coolers feature refreezable bottles of non-toxic ice substitutes that screw into cooler lids or are otherwise designed to lie above food. The containers can also be refrozen as needed and generally last as long as ice and sometimes longer.

Keep the cooler out of the sun at all times, and on really hot days cover it with a white towel that is wet. Keep the drain plug closed, and don't open the cooler any more than necessary and then as briefly as possible. Save the cardboard box that held your cooler when you bought it. The cardboard, along with newspaper stuffed in the corners and anywhere else there is air space, will help ice last.

When packing your cooler, store first those items needed last so they will remain on bottom where it is coolest. On long fishing and hunting trips, I layer my cooler bottom with frozen meat, which I wrap in newspaper to double the length of time needed to thaw it. Consider using two coolers, one large and one small, and then each morning transfer those items needed for the day. That way, ice will last much longer in the bigger cooler.

More tips: Block ice stays frozen longer than crushed type, and clear block ice melts more slowly than milky ice. You can even make your own block ice at home by freezing water in empty milk cartons. Green bananas and tomatoes will ripen in camp. To speed the process, store them in a sunny spot or seal tightly in plastic bags—the gas that emits will do the rest.

PREPARING NUTRITIOUS MEALS

Many campers and some backpackers pay little attention to the nutritional value of the foods they eat. That's too bad because (1) you need a lot of energy to take on the outdoors, (2) planning and preparing nutritious meals could save your life.

The Importance of Energy-Producing Foods

Body energy comes from three fuel sources: foods high in protein, carbohydrates and fat. Proteins are cell builders, providing heat and energy for the body. Lean meats and raw nuts are high in protein. Carbohydrates containing sugar, starch or cellulose (candy bars, noodles, potatoes) give

Packing in the carbohydrates in deer hunting camp, these hunters know it will be a cold day tomorrow.

quick energy. Fats, on the other hand, provide reserves for long-term energy needs. Peanut butter, bacon and some cheeses are examples.

Fats yield 9.3 calories per gram, as compared to 4.0 calories per gram for carbohydrates and 4.1 calories per gram for protein. What do these statistics mean to campers and backpackers? Depending upon the stress level of expected activity, they should plan meals with an eye to the energy-producing value of what they eat.

Any good cookbook contains easy-to-fix recipes high in energy. A little imagination will turn up others. The truth is whatever you enjoy cooking and, more importantly, whatever you like to eat, can be made in camp. Considerations include:

Trail mix, or gorp, can be made on the spot and taken along on the trail for high-energy snacks throughout the day.

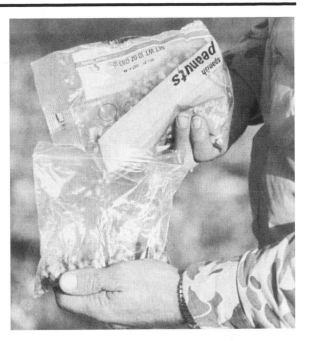

1. Time (campers on the go can't wait for Bean Hole Beans).

2. Experience (don't try new recipes in camp—practice at home first).

3. Weight and Space (how much room do you have; how much can you comfortably tote?).

4. Cleanup (you're a long way from a dishwasher).

5. Heat Source (how much fuel do you have, and how even is the flame?).

A typical quick breakfast for me consists of instant oatmeal topped with raisins, brown sugar and a pinch of cinnamon. A wedge of cheese, granola bar, handful of sunflower seeds, or packet of raisins or peanuts gives me a quick burst of energy. Sometimes I'll mix the goodies together to make trail mix or what some backpackers still call "gorp."

I'm a bacon-and-eggs, meat-and-potatoes kind of eater, but the outdoor trails I follow do not often allow time or the necessary conveniences for preparing fancy meals. In spite of the high fat content of some of the quick-fix things I eat, I don't gain weight. That's because the canoeing, backpacking and other activities I pursue eat up calories as fast as I can supply them.

A word about freeze-dried foods: They are expensive, often costing

Freeze-dried foods are popular with backpackers who want to cut weight and have foods quick and easy to prepare. The bear-proof food container is made by Garcia Machine Co.

NUTRITIONAL VALUE OF FOODS CAMPERS LOVE

Food Type	Amount	Calories	Protein	Fat	Carbohydrate
Oatmeal (cooked)	1 cup	148	5.4	2.6	26.0
Cornmeal (cooked)	1 cup	119	2.4	0.5	25.5
Buttermilk biscuit	1	82	1.5	4.1	9.2
Whole wheat bread	1 slice	56	2.4	0.7	11.0
White bread	1 slice	62	2.0	0.7	11.6
Pancakes	1 (avg.)	104	3.2	3.2	15.3
Orange juice	2/5 cup	45	0.7	0.2	10.4
Special K cereal	1 cup	76	4.2	—	14.6
Total cereal	1 cup	109	3.0	1.0	22.7
Sugar Crisps	1 cup	121	2.3	0.4	28.6
Bacon	1/4 lb.	712	0.3	73.6	1.2
Cured ham	3.5 ozs.	348	22.5	28.0	0.3
Sausage links	3.5 ozs.	450	10.8	44.8	—
Milk (evap.)	1 cup	352	17.6	20.0	24.8
Eggs (fried)	1 egg	108	6.2	8.6	0.4
Omelette	1 med.	107	7.2	8.0	1.7
Spaghetti	1 cup	166	5.1	0.6	34.4
Lasagna	1 serv.	310	14.0	9.0	44.0

double or more the price of do-it-yourself prepared foods. They taste fine, are light as a bag of potato chips, and are wonderfully convenient. An hour after eating them, though, I'm hungry (remember the old joke about eating Chinese food?), and I don't seem to get the lasting energy I need. I might pack a few items of freeze-dried food, but I don't rely on them for all my meals.

All counties in the United States have a cooperative extension services agency staffed with a trained home economist. You can call to get information about your favorite foods, pamphlets on nutrition, and other items of interest to campers. They're available for free or a nominal charge. Here is what I learned about some common foods that campers love (protein, fat and carbohydrate yields are in grams):

Food Type	Amount	Calories	Protein	Fat	Carbohydrate
Meat loaf	3.5 ozs.	160	17.0	7.6	4.6
Chipped beef	1/2 cup	209	16.1	13.0	6.1
Hamburger	1 patty	140	25.9	3.4	—
Beef stew (can)	1 cup	204	15.0	8.0	18.3
Tuna noodle dish	1 cup	280	17.8	11.8	25.0
Hash browns	1/2 cup	229	3.1	11.7	29.1
Chili	5 ozs.	200	10.3	14.8	5.8
Chocolate pudding	1/2 cup	163	3.9	3.9	31.7
Raisins (plain)	1 tbsp.	29	0.3	—	7.7
Raisins (choc.)	1 oz.	119	1.5	4.8	19.7
Granola	1 bar	210	6.0	10.0	24.0
Snickers	1 bar	159	3.4	6.2	22.4
M&M candy	35 grms.	177	4.2	8.9	20.0
Hershey bar	1 oz.	155	2.6	9.3	15.1
Sunflower seeds	3.5 ozs.	560	24.0	47.3	19.9
Peanut butter	1 tbsp.	86	3.9	7.2	3.2
Peanuts	2.5 ozs.	572	26.5	46.7	22.0
Beef jerky	10 grms.	36	4.2	1.7	1.4

CAMPING WITH KIDS

Camping is the perfect activity for family members to spend quality time together. Gone are the stresses of job and school. Absent are the distraction of friends and social commitments. You just have each other now—Mom, Dad and the kids. During a single week of camping, you may see more of your children close-up than you have for many weeks prior to leaving home.

Involving children in the planning stage teaches them organizational skills and makes them feel an important part of the family camping trip.

To make the most of this opportunity, give some thought to how human relationships will be tested. What lessons do you hope to both learn and impart? What are the expectations of your spouse and kids? Tip: A weekend camping trip or even a single overnighter before the family vacation will tell you much about your children's abilities and what to expect from them. Smoother relationships will result on longer trips.

Letting Youngsters in on the Plan

Kids should be involved in every step of the camping trip from planning to execution to Monday-morning quarterbacking on the drive home. The best way to find out what your youngsters' interests are is to include them in the planning. Assuming the kids are old enough, have them write letters for information to travel bureaus, chambers of commerce and state and provincial tourism departments. If the kids are too young, write the letters in their name, then make a big deal out of the personal mail they receive.

Now is a good opportunity to teach children map reading and orientation, too. A trip or two to the library for books, magazines and other camping information further helps involve them. At age ten, my son was allowed to plan a portion of our 8,600-mile, six-week trip out West. He devised the travel route, the day's itinerary, and chose the campground. As an adult today he is one of the most efficient planners I know, and I like to think I had something to do with that.

Sharing the Load

As both a parent and a former public schoolteacher, I know that children nearly always live up to the expectations we have of them. I also know that kids expect and want responsibilities, but for many parents it's hard to judge how much to give them. You can help solve this problem in camp by making a checklist of jobs that need doing. Every family member takes turns choosing what he or she wants to be responsible for.

On another long trip my son's first choice was to clean the truck windshield and check the engine oil daily. My daughter, five years younger, opted for emptying the litter basket and sweeping the truck floor each morning. If any of us, adults included, forgot our assigned chores or became lax, the truck didn't leave the campground. Soon, each of us knew the importance of our jobs. The only way to get rid of one task was to trade it for someone else's.

Letting the Kids Cook

The responsibilities you give children should be commensurate with their maturity and readiness levels. For example, my wife and I taught our adolescent children to cook at an early age. Why not? They have to learn sometime and what better place than in a campground, miles from Mom's sparkling kitchen? Every child loves toasting marshmallows and making s'mores over an open fire. If you think they're ready to graduate to the real thing, they will love it and live up to your expectation. Once again, we involved the kids in the planning stage. As I recall, they were quite practical, remembering to pack things that we might have otherwise forgotten.

We started with simple menus. For breakfast, hot cereal and fruit. Later we let the kids graduate to French toast and scrambled eggs. First lunches

Letting kids plan and prepare a meal, under adult supervision, teaches them responsibility.

can be soup heated from a can or powder mixed with hot water, along with tuna fish sandwiches, barbecued beef or sloppy Joes. Suppers of beans and franks, hamburgers, goulash and spaghetti are easy to fix.

Another idea is to prepare and freeze foods such as chili, fried chicken, Salisbury steak, beef stew, Spanish rice, tuna noodle casserole and meat loaf before leaving home. Thawing and heating over the campstove will provide a quick and easy meal and is an ideal way to break a youngster into the art of culinary expression.

The question of safety is always in the minds of many parents who consider letting their kids cook. The concern may or may not be justified—no one knows your children like you. Certainly some supervision is in order, which may be increased or lessened depending upon how the kids handle themselves.

Several suggestions can help ease the fear of hazard, though. If kids are to cook over an open fire, consider the Sterno stove, a one- or two-burner device that uses canned heat, is non-explosive and non-melting, and is considered quite safe. Even so, keep an eye out and a fire extinguisher handy. If cooking indoors, make certain that proper ventilation is available, that foods (greasy ones in particular) are cooked slowly, and that propane burners are turned off when finished. Minor burns from hot skillets are part of the trial-and-error dangers all cooks must face. Keeping a first aid kit handy is always a must, no matter who does the cooking. Storing food in plastic rather than glass containers is a good safety idea, too.

Giving Children Personal Space

Especially when there are siblings to compete, children want a place to call their own. It may be the car seat by the window, or the sleeping pad near the tent door. Giving them a personal spot and making sure they have their own duffel bag and souvenir container help them to have an identify and place within the family.

Teaching Limits

Enforce the same rules that apply at home: picking up after themselves, tending to personal hygiene, going to bed at the appointed hour. If you

Happy campers come in all ages and sizes. These kids were given their own tent to play and sleep in.

do relax the rules, make sure the child understands why.

Camping and traveling is also a good time to teach a youngster the value of money and how to budget it. Weeks before your camping vacation make the kids save a portion of their allowance, then—depending on their relative maturity—make them responsible for spending it wisely. On that six-week-long camping trip, my kids had amassed what would be about $200 and $150 respectively in today's dollars. When my son ran out of money a week from home and my daughter had her untended purse relieved of $20, both childern knew better than to ask for an advance on their allowance. It always was a cruel world, wasn't it?

Learning to Respect Others

Kids don't instinctively share but they can learn to do so on a camping trip. Scouting activities are one of the best ways to learn sharing, cooperation and respect for others and the environment. Family camping is another tremendous opportunity. Here are some dos and don'ts to instill in your charges (and to remind yourself of periodically):

Letting kids carry a light pack appropriate for their age teaches them self-re-liance and develops fitness.

• Offer to help camping neighbors with chores such as setting up the tent and gathering water. Take your cues from their reaction—some people camp to get away from others, even nice folks like you and your family.

• Be willing to share what you have with others. A cup of coffee and token gift of firewood are greatly appreciated and remembered.

• Be quiet during quiet hours, giving others the same privacy you would like. Don't shortcut, for example, through another camper's site.

• Don't hog all the hot water in the communal shower.

• Leave your campsite cleaner than you found it. How about a token bundle of firewood? You might even build a ready-to-light campfire in the fire ring, along with a note asking the next fellow to be equally considerate.

• Don't pick wildflowers or chop live trees. Stay on trails and observe other posted campground regulations.

• Don't clean dishes or fish in lakes and rivers. Properly dispose of all refuse.

Finding Fun Things to Do

When kids get bored, they become restless and often create problems for other family members. Parents are not responsible for their children's boredom. Still, there are things to do to help pass the time when traveling or when everyone is stuck in the tent on a rainy day.

• Pack playing cards and board games. Also, encourage the kids to bring appropriate reading material and suggest that they keep a diary or journal of their trip.

• Carry some mind teasers, puzzles or dexterity games in the glove box or day pack.

• Play Charades or Password or make up games like "I'm thinking of a state (or state capitol, country, city, item in a supermarket, etc.) that begins with the letter M". Auto bingo that uses landmarks and road signs instead of numbers is fun to play. So are out-of-state license plate games.

• Carry a jug of ice water and styrofoam cups, and a pocketful of roll candy.

• If traveling, stop often and let the kids work off a little energy.

CAMPING WITH PETS

Traveling and camping with your pet makes sense these days. After all, a four-legged companion at home can also be a pal on the road or in the campground. What's more, you can save $10 or more per day on boarding fees.

If you follow a few guidelines, you won't have to worry about your pet's welfare. One key consideration is the animal's behavior. Some dogs and cats travel as calmly as a veteran, first-class passenger. Others get carsick, leave messy paw prints on windows, deposit surprises in the back seat, and require a general sedative before they settle down.

You'll also want to be certain your pet is welcome wherever you plan to stay. Some campgrounds accept animals, but others do not. Traveling and camping with a pet can be a good or a bad experience. It's mostly up to you. Here are some considerations to make sure your experience is a good one:

• Stop every couple of hours to let your pet exercise and relieve itself.

• Keep the pet on a leash at all times to protect it and others from harm. You can't always predict what an animal will do, especially when it has been cooped up in a car and is now in unfamilar surroundings.

• If your dog snaps at strangers or bays at the moon, buy a strong leash and a muzzle, too. If your cat is the nervous type, clip its nails.

• Carry a current health certificate indicating date of rabies and other shots. Such a doctor-signed statement is required for foreign and airline travel.

Camping with a pet won't create problems if you follow a few simple guidelines.

The author takes at least one, and sometimes all four, of his dogs on most camping trips.

• Consider any health needs. Always carry cool water, heartworm pills and basic first aid, including a mild antiseptic. Will your female's heat cycle cause problems? Does the pet need a mild tranquilizer?

• Plan for comfortable sleeping arrangements. Bringing a familiar pillow, blanket or sleeping box may help the pet orientate itself to new surroundings.

• Avoid feeding the pet before traveling. Meeting strangers and riding in a car to new places can easily stress a fed animal.

• Don't change your pet's diet while on the road. When you arrive at your destination, calm the animal and give it a small amount of water and a taste of familiar food.

• Don't leave the pet locked in the car, trunk, tent or trailer for hours on end without supervision and proper ventilation. Temperatures in a locked vehicle can soar to 140 degrees on a hot summer day. Some unattended pets become destructive out of nervous energy.

• Don't forget to bring a collar with your pet's name, your name, address and phone number. Be sure to carry the animal's license and registration numbers in case you must identify it if lost, injured or stolen. Color photographs may help you to find and identify a lost pet.

COPING WITH CAMP PESTS

Camping encounters with wildlife are the exception, not the rule. In a lifetime of sleeping outdoors, I have experienced perhaps a half-dozen incidents, all of which could have been avoided with the exception of a foraging grizzly bear in the arctic. I awakened one night to a rough panting outside our tiny tent. In a panic I found my .44 magnum handgun and ripped it from its holster. Holding a shaking penlight in my mouth, I sat up in my sleeping bag, the gun in both trembling hands, and waited for a certain attack.

Luckily, the bear was merely curious. Finding nothing to eat, he wandered off into the dark, but I was too shook up to sleep anymore that night.

The fear of wild animals is a big reason why many people who don't camp are not interested in trying the experience. I asked this question of

Normally shy wild animals often become emboldened in camp-grounds because they know people are a source of food.

several noncampers at a house party recently. One woman said the last time she camped, a fellow Girl Scout dropped a garter snake into her sleeping bag. "I'll never go camping again, if I live to be a hundred," she insisted. Another person indicated that his cousin's family suffered an ordeal with a skunk while camping the previous summer.

"So take the family dog along for protection," someone else offered.

"They did," he admitted. "It was their poodle who caught the skunk in the tent and got sprayed. They had to cut their camping vacation short."

Avoiding Bears

Foraging bears are a constant threat to campers in the backcountry and in many of our national parks. The last time I visited Yellowstone, rangers drove throughout the campground each evening, warning people to put food away. In Glacier National Park a couple of years ago a black bear surprised my wife and me as we hiked along a trail back to our camp. The bruin, more interested in berries than in us, ambled off the path into the woods.

My arctic camping partner and I avoided a confrontation with that curious grizzly because we had taken certain precautions. We prepared and ate supper 50 yards from our tent. We washed dishes, stuffed empty food packaging into Ziploc bags, and made doubly certain that no food or food odors lingered in the area. Had trees been available, we would have suspended our mess kits and food supplies on a rope 15 feet above the ground and at least 5 feet from the tree trunk. We even changed clothes before climbing into our sleeping bags. That left nothing to smell except human beings, and when the bear got a whiff of us, he "woofed" and left camp in a hurry.

"A fed bear is a dead bear" say the posters in our Western national parks. A bear that is rewarded only once by finding food in a campground quickly loses its fear of people. That bear will have to be removed. If it becomes a problem, park personnel will kill the animal.

Many government-run parks provide food lockers in modern campgrounds and food poles or cables in backcountry ones to keep chow away from bears. Auto campers are required to lock all food in the trunks of cars at night and to dispose of trash in bear-proof receptacles provided. Besides these precautions, there are many other things campers can do to avoid a confrontation with a bear.

Foraging bears—make that people who feed bears—are the number one problem in some campgrounds.

• Don't hike alone or after dark, and whistle, sing or otherwise make loud noises when traveling through known bear country. A bear that hears you will nearly always move off the trail.

• If you see a cub, back off; never get between a cub and its mother.

• Stay as clean as possible, avoid scented shampoos and deodorants, and don't sleep in the clothes you wore all day and cooked in. Instead, hang them away from camp, along with your food.

• Remember that a tent affords more protection than sleeping in the open. Keep a flashlight and a noisemaker handy.

• Most importantly, don't provoke a bear by approaching the animal for photos or a better look. According to the National Park Service, if you run into a bear, avoid eye contact (which might be interpreted as a threat), talk softly and walk away, while dropping something that might distract the bear.

Veteran hunters, fishermen and campers often carry a cut-down shotgun with slugs or buckshot or a powerful sidearm when traveling through bear country. Counter Assault, a can of eye and lung irritant

Grizzly bears can run up to 35 mph, faster than a horse, and should never be approached. The author photographed this Alaska grizzly with a 400mm lens.

similar to mace that comes complete with holster, is touted to repel grizzlies at a distance of 18 to 50 feet. If you are attacked and have no means of defense, however, the best advice—according to the NPS—is to drop to the ground, assume the fetal position so the knees will protect vital organs, cover your head with your arms, and play dead.

Other Camp Critters

At best, the occasional camp pest is a simple nuisance. At worst, they are downright dangerous. Mice, chipmunks, pack rats and squirrels are naturally attracted to shelters but will do no harm if they find nothing to eat. They are as friendly and fun to have around as those noisy camp robbers, the Canada jays, who are likewise drawn to shiny objects and pose no real threat if you operate and maintain a clean camp.

That is also the key to avoiding problems with skunks, raccoons and porcupines, all of which are easily suckered into camp by the odor of bacon grease and other powerful smells. Properly dispose of garbage and put away all food. Most nocturnal camp pests can be scared off with a flashlight and noisemaker.

However, small animals may bite campers who try to pick them up.

When threatened, skunks and porcupines defend with tools other than tooth and claw. Always avoid a direct confrontation, and walk away from any emboldened animal—it could be rabid.

Biting Insects

As mentioned earlier, the best way to avoid mosquitoes and black flies is not to set up camp near their habitat. The same is true for bees, ticks, no-see-ums and other gnats, deer flies, sand flies and, in the South, chiggers and fire ants. Further protection tactics for these and other biting insects include daily inspection of your clothes and body, washing with no-odor shampoo and soap, avoiding perfume and cologne, and keeping handy a good repellent containing plenty of DEET. Be certain your first-aid kit contains an anti-sting product, and make sure no one in your party is allergic to bee stings. If so, consult a doctor for the right prescription medicine.

Apparently biting insects hone in on victims through sensory perception, and some tests suggest that the body odors of lactic acid and exhala-

A Canada jay (whiskey jack) helps himself to table leavings at a campground in the Yukon Territory.

tion of carbon dioxide actually draw them. Repellents seem to be the best way to jam an insect's sensors, but even then they don't always work.

What *does* repel insects? The U.S. Government began testing during WW II to find out because malaria and yellow fever were killing our soldiers in the Tropics. By 1951 scientists had tested some 11,000 compounds. A few, such as oil of citronella, were effective. Most weren't. Then eventually researchers discovered DEET, short for N, N-Diethyl-meta-toluamide. Nothing has come along since to better it (although Avon Skin-So-Soft—especially when cut with rubbing alcohol—and Johnson's Off! Skintastic work for awhile on some people and have a pleasant odor). The last time I looked, Deep Woods Off! contained 30 percent DEET, Cutter's cream formula had 50 percent DEET, Muskol lotion contained 95 percent DEET, and Ben's 100 was 100 percent DEET.

The more DEET the better, except for one thing: the chemical compound attacks plastic and can ruin a watch crystal and turn your fishing reel into a sticky mess. In fact, health experts are now beginning to look at DEET with suspicion. Any chemical that powerful can't be safe is the theory.

My body must not produce an inordinate amount of lactic acid because, for the most part, black flies and mosquitoes leave me alone. Others, like my wife, are constantly annoyed and so must apply copious amounts of repellent, some of which now come with sunscreen, or wear a headnet.

Mud packs and body rubs with grease and tallow were used by campers before our time. Others placed herbs around their tents, ate huge quantities of garlic (some people still do and others load up with vitamin B) and concocted home remedies of oil of citronella, pine oil, gum camphor, stearic acid and oil of pennyroyal. Smudge fires of ferns (a natural source of citronella oil), electric bug zappers and citronella candles are other deterrents to try although to my mind they are more of a nuisance than the insects themselves. If all else fails, consider staying in campgrounds that are chemically treated for insects.

Poisonous Snakes

I have never encountered poisonous snakes but know of other campers who have. Once again, the prescription is avoidance. In Western grasslands, stay away from prairie dog towns; in desert areas, avoid pack rat burrows; elsewhere, don't set up camp near swamps or other low-lying areas.

LEAVING NO TRACE

Environmental scars can last a long time. Riding through an aspen grove in Nevada's Ruby Mountains one fall, friends and I paused to let our horses graze. I was surprised to discover that a spate of graffiti, carved into a tree trunk in 1934, was still legible. Look about you the next time you go camping: Trampled trails, eroded stream banks, and tin cans, plastic and other nonbiodegradable litter are grim evidence that a thoughtless person came before. Just when we think we've found an untouched pocket of wilderness, blackened rocks and half-burned logs from a careless campfire too often tell a different story.

As more people turn to the outdoors for recreation, the negative impact they make on the environment increases. According to Tread Lightly! Inc., a group trying to minimize land abuse through responsible use of off-highway vehicles, 42 percent of U.S. Forest Service lands have been restricted or closed in the past 15 years. Yellowstone, Glacier and other national parks are overrun by too many people who either don't know how to lessen their impact or don't care enough to try.

Yet minimum-impact or no-trace camping is growing in popularity. The goal of many campers and backpackers is to leave nothing behind but an occasional footprint. They are not crazed environmentalists; they are concerned citizens who want to contribute to a healthier environment for themselves and future generations. Here are ways you can become a more considerate camper:

Merge, Don't Purge

Adopt the attitude that your journey into the outdoors is to enjoy what the land has to offer without changing it. That means using environmentally friendly products like no-rinse soap for bathing and clean-burning stoves. Foam sleeping pads eliminate the need for gathering evergreen boughs for bedding. Waterproof tents with sewn-in floors end the often harmful practice of digging trenches around the tent.

Think Minimum, Not Maximum

Planning for a qualitative, rather than a quantitative, experience is the key to no-trace camping. Consider gear: Shovels, axes and chain saws, although perhaps necessary in a destination camp, are not tools required by most campers anymore. One of camping's joys is the campfire at night, but why build a raging bonfire when a small blaze of light is equally satisfying? Portable shower bags and plastic water containers minimize the amount of water used and preclude the need to camp at the water source. Use a trowel to dig a small cat hole instead of a shovel to make a big latrine.

Fires and Cooking

If you build a fire, locate it away from ground vegetation and also large rocks. Use your trowel to remove a small chunk of sod, scatter the cooled ashes, then replace the sod when you leave. Thoroughly burn only downed and dead wood, making sure to leave no charred ends for someone to find. Sift through the fire to remove any debris, then pack it out.

Cooking with propane, butane or white gas is cleaner and faster than making meals over an open fire. Utensils clean up more easily, too. Use boiling water (no soap) for doing the dishes. A handful of sand or scour rush (horse weeds, we used to call them) will clean a skillet as well as detergent.

Other Considerations

• Camp at least 200 feet from your water source, don't wash dishes there, and vary your approach so as to protect stream banks and vegetation.

• Spread out, rather than follow each other, when hiking in high country and over other fragile areas. That way you'll avoid trampling plant life, especially in the high country, which leads to erosion and may take a generation to heal. On established trails, stick to the center and travel single file.

• Pack out everything you pack in.

Ultralight back-packing lanterns and stoves preclude the need for campfires in the backcountry.

• Keep pets leashed and under control.

• Scatter dirty water over the ground rather than dump it into a stream or lake.

• Always get a permit if camping outside established campgrounds. The permit system, when it is practiced, helps spreads people pressure.

As more people adopt the minimum-impact concept, an increasing number of companies are now making tents, packs and other gear in earth-tone colors that blend into the landscape. For more suggestions contact the National Outdoor Leadership School, 288 Main, Lander, WY 82520 (307-332-6973), and ask for information about their Leave No Trace program.

DEALING WITH HEALTH EMERGENCIES

Even the best-laid plans for a camping vacation can be ruined if possible mishaps and unexpected illness away from home are not considered. A few minutes of planning will help avoid a night lost sitting in an emergency room in a strange town or a half-day's wait in a doctor's office—assuming you can acquire medical help in an emergency.

The First-Aid Kit

I have two first-aid kits, and I don't venture outdoors without one or the other. The first is very basic and small and can be carried in a shirt

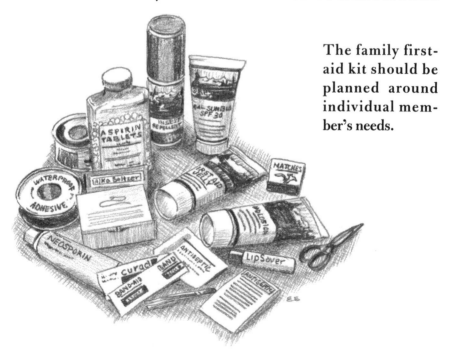

The family first-aid kit should be planned around individual member's needs.

pocket, car glove box or backpack. It contains an antiseptic cream, Band-Aids in various sizes, needles, a pair of tweezers, a half-dozen aspirin tablets, magnifying glass and tick-removal tool, eye drops, lip balm, antacid tablets and a couple of squares of gauze. It's great for treating blisters from hiking or cooking, dressing simple cuts, removing splinters and other pesky but nonlife-threatening problems.

The other kit is more elaborate—it cost about $100—and we raid it occasionally at home as well as take it along for overnight camping trips. Weighing less than three pounds, the Trekker II is made by Atwater Carey, who designed its contents of 163 items to handle emergencies and medical needs of four to six people traveling for up to two months. A thermometer, scissors, disposable rubber gloves and specialty Blood-stopper trauma dressings are included. There's stuff in there that I don't know how to use, but I could read the manual provided and someone else with medical training would know instantly. I feel confident whenever I have this kit along.

You can make your own first-aid kit and save money by buying supplies from a discount pharmacy and making your own container. A fruit cake tin, shortening can, plastic food storage container, child's school lunch pail, cosmetic bag or ammo box are suggestions to consider. A miniaturized first-aid kit can be assembled in a metal Band-Aid box, a recipe box or small plastic container. Common problems you may face outdoors and items to pack in the kit include:

• Minor burns (including sunburn)—a mild spray antiseptic.

• Minor cuts, scratches—an antiseptic, various sizes of Band-Aids, 4 × 4 gauze pads.

• Insect bites—antiseptic ointment or spray. Tick-removal tool.

•Poisonous plants—lotion containing calamine, camphor and/or benadryl (a prescription drug).

• Poisonous snakes—a snake-bite kit from Sawyer Products or another company.

• Pain—aspirin (adult, children), ibuprofin, aspirin substitutes such as Tylenol.

• Nausea—antacids (Pepto-Bismol or Alka-Seltzer)

• Diarrhea—Kaopectate.

• Foot blisters—moleskin or Spenco Second Skin, clean socks, antiseptic, gauze pads, adhesive tape.

• Irregularity—laxatives, anti-diarrheics.

Packing an all-around skin cleanser like Betadine, which contains a mild antiseptic, is as important as Band-Aids.

• Sprains, bruises—chemical coldpack, elastic bandage, adhesive tape.

• Sore muscles—analgesic (Ben-Gay, Heet, etc.) rubbing alcohol.

Be sure to pack scissors, tweezers, safety pins, needles, a single-edge razor blade, a space blanket, waterproof matches (for sterilizing tools), fingernail clippers, thermometer, eye drops, cough medicine, decongestant and any prescription medicines, including an approved antibiotic. Never leave home without a health insurance card and the name and phone number of your doctor.

First-Aid Procedures

The most important thing anyone can do for an injured or ill person is to keep calm and in control. Even if you do not know what to do, do not panic. Your behavior can easily intensify the victim's emotional state, causing fear and panic, which can produce hyperventilation and additional bleeding. If you do not know what to do, do nothing. Send someone for help or seek it yourself if you are the only other person at the scene.

Cuts

Because most immediate first-aid applications are basic, they require only coolness and common sense. For a cut, wash the area thoroughly with warm water and wash gently in mild soap suds. Warm water is also effective if soap is not available. If the cut is slight, apply a spray or liquid antiseptic and cover with a Band-Aid or piece of clean gauze and adhesive tape.

For deep cuts, gentle washing will help keep debris out, but do not apply ointments or antiseptics. Try to protect the area with clean bandages for the trip to the hospital or doctor's office. If the cut needs suturing, seek medical attention as soon as possible. The longer the wait, the greater the chance for infection. A tetanus shot will be required for all injured persons who have not had one within five years. However, a tetanus shot must be administered within 72 hours of injury.

Bleeding

Bleeding can usually be controlled by applying steady pressure to the wound for three minutes or more. A tourniquet should be used only as a last resort.

Serious Problems

For serious problems such as a broken bone, concussion or internal injury, do not move the victim more than necessary until the extent of the damage can be determined. When moving is required, do everything possible to hold the injured sections still, and keep the limbs and back in alignment. The latter is extremely important for suspected neck or back injuries. If you must, tentatively splint a suspected break to keep that part of the body immobile.

Suspected Sprains

For suspected sprains apply ice or cold water for the first 24 hours, at intervals, to reduce swelling. A chemical cold pack may be used or the injured part dunked in a pail of cold water. Elevate the injured limb to help fluids drain out of the muscle tissue. After 24 hours heat is helpful—not before. Heat may be applied dry (a heating pad or hot-water bottle) or wet (a wash cloth soaked in hot water). You can make an ice bag or hot-water bottle from a Ziploc bag or cloth-wrapped jar. Wrapping ice cubes in a wash cloth is another way to make a quick cold pack.

Loss of Consciousness

A person who has fainted should be lowered to the ground and his feet elevated. Wipe the victim's face with a damp cloth. When revived, do not allow the person to stand up quickly.

Skin Irritations

Poison ivy, poison oak, poison sumac, nettles, insect bites and other skin allergies may require medical attention but seldom require emergency

Leaves three, let it be! Poison ivy grows in many places campers visit.

treatment. Washing the affected area with warm water and mild soap can relieve much of the discomfort. Do not allow water to run over unaffected areas, or the problem might spread. If irritation continues, a spray antiseptic or lotions or creams containing a steroid can be applied.

Buy a good all-around antiseptic effective for minor abrasions, cuts, skin irritations and burns. There is no reason to carry a half-dozen antiseptics when one will do the job.

Insect Bites

In addition to preventions and repellents already mentioned, treat bee stings and insect bites with an anti-sting lotion available from any pharmacy. You can make a paste from meat tenderizer (like Adolph's) or baking soda and water.

Use a tweezers and magnifying glass to remove stingers. If you have been bitten by a tick, touch a hot matchhead to the spot and hope the insect backs out (the same trick sometimes works with bloodsuckers that have attached themselves to swimmers). Take care in removing the tick because gorged body parts can break easily and you'll be left with head and pincers inside your skin where they could spread venom or infection.

Burns and Blisters

First-degree burns are the least serious—they cause reddening of the skin and minor pain. Second-degree burns develop blisters, and third-degree burns result in deep tissue destruction and are very serious. First- and second-degree burns may be treated with cold water and an antiseptic spray. Third-degree burns need professional attention as soon as possible.

The best first-aid treatment for any burn is immediate immersion in cold water. This action helps relieve some of the pain and can prevent a bad burn from becoming worse. If immersion is not possible, douse the area with whatever cold liquid is at hand—a glass of iced tea, for example.

Remove all clothing that comes off easily. If fabric material sticks to the skin, do not try to remove the clothing. Gently cover the burnt area with a clean dressing (sterile, if possible). A clean towel, handkerchief or shirt tail can be used if that is all that is available. Never put ointments, antiseptics, creams or lotions on a severe burn. Do not apply butter or grease to any burn because they do not relieve pain and could complicate healing through a bad infection.

Treat blisters caused from poor-fitting shoes or boots by cleaning the feet, then applying an antiseptic and gauze bandage. At the first sign of chafing, put a piece of moleskin over the affected area. If hiking, change socks every few hours and footwear every day if possible.

Nausea, Fever, Diarrhea

These problems can usually be treated with nonprescriptive medicines. However, if a problem persists for more than 24 hours, seek medical attention. A complication of diarrhea is dehydration (loss of bodily fluids), which can be especially troublesome for young children. Tip: To avoid contracting diarrhea, rinse dishes clean of soap and drink only clean water.

Altitude affects backpackers differently. Early signs are a headache and slight nosebleed. Especially when hiking with children, be on the lookout for altitude sickness. Rest often; descend if conditions persist.

Altitude Sickness

The condition occurs in high country and can affect people at differing levels of elevation. Symptoms are shortness of breath, fatigue, headache, nausea and bloody nose. Drinking lots of water, thinning the blood through aspirin, and eating antacid tablets will help prevent altitude sickness. But until the body has time to make more red blood cells, a process which can take up to 10 days, there is nothing else to do except venture into high country gradually and rest often. If symptoms are severe, descend to a lower altitude.

Choking

Choking victims may be aided by a few hard slaps on the back. If that action doesn't help, stand behind the person and grasp him so that your fists are under his breastbone. Then pull suddenly in an upward and inward motion so that the pressure can dislodge anything caught in his throat.

Drowning or Suspected Heart Attack

Whenever breathing stops or a heart attack is suspected, quick action is necessary. The best prevention is in taking a course in cardiopulmonary resuscitation. Classes in CPR are offered nationally by the American Red Cross and numerous other hospital-affiliated groups.

Hypothermia

Hypothermia is the rapid loss of body temperature due to exposure to cold, and is the number one killer of outdoor enthusiasts. It occurs most frequently in both water and air temperatures between 30 and 50 degrees. Make the victim as warm as possible by wrapping him in a space blanket or sleeping bag, slipping a knit cap over his head, and quickly changing him into dry clothes. Try to keep the person awake, and give him sips of warm liquids.

Hyperthermia

Hyperthermia is somewhat the reverse condition of hypothermia—body temperature usually rises from overexposure to heat. The conditions of heat exhaustion and heat stroke are related to hyperthermia. A person suffering from heat exhaustion will sweat profusely, though his temperature remains the same. A heat stroke victim, on the other hand, does not sweat but his temperature rises, and he may go into shock.

Victims of either condition should be placed in the shade and cooled down by removing as much clothing as possible. For heat exhaustion give the person cool water to drink with one or two teaspoons of salt added per quart.

A person in shock will have a weak, thready pulse, his pupils may dilate, his complexion may pale, and he may even be unconscious. Until professional help arrives, lay him flat with his feet elevated about one foot. Try to maintain body temperature—if cold to the touch—by covering with a blanket or jacket, taking care to keep something between the victim and the cold ground. Apply pressure to any bleeding wound.

Individual Health Needs

It cannot be overemphasized—anyone planning a first-aid kit should consider the health needs of each family member. Prescribed medicine (tablets and pills are preferred over spillable liquids) should be labeled and carried in their drug store containers. Allergy and blood-type information should be entered on index cards—one for each family member—and carried in the kit.

Packing specific medical information while camping in South Dakota a few years ago literally saved my neck. A rough boat ride on the Missouri River put my neck out of joint. For years in my wallet I had carried the alignment figures and other information that my chiropractor uses to set things straight at home. I used the tattered card for the first time, and a Rapid City chiropractor was able to correct my condition without expensive, time-consuming Xrays.

Another good tip is to carry the same prescribed medicine in two separate containers, in two separate locations—perhaps the first-aid kit and a locked glove box. A friend of mine with a heart condition once left his small first-aid kit containing nitro-glycerine tablets atop his car in a remote area. His medicine lost and the camping trip spoiled, my friend had to return home. Now he carries his medicine in two containers to prevent losing more than half at any time.

LIVING OFF THE LAND

Traveling by vehicle affords campers a great opportunity to sample fresh fruits and vegetables purchased from roadside stands. If you know how to distinguish wild edibles from dangerous plants and fruits, collecting your own fresh table fare can add a fun dimension to camping. Wild fruit tastes great with cereal, and how about sautéing the trout you caught with fresh morel mushrooms? Tip: Pick up a good pocket identification guide such as *Color Field Guide to Common Wild Edibles* by Bradford Angier (Stackpole Books).

No weed killers or insecticides taint natural plants, and no artificial flavorings or coloring contaminate the taste of wild fruit. Preservatives are absent, too. Here are a few tasty wild foods to watch for:

Mushrooms are one of many wild edibles that campers can enjoy, provided they know what they are picking.

Wild Strawberries

You may smell them before you see the tiny, scarlet fruit poking out from small three-leaf clusters low to the ground. Wild strawberries grow in open fields, fence rows, burned-over areas, and dry, open woods. Identify them by white flowers in late May and early June. Fruit ripens in June and July. The late naturalist, Euell Gibbons, once called them "the top prize for the wild food gatherer."

Blueberries

You can't miss these dark blue-black berries with sometimes a whitish bloom about them. Both low-bush and high-bush varieties prefer sandy or rocky soil in upland areas, and they thrive on short, stiff bushes 10 to 20 inches high. Burned-over areas are excellent haunts. In just two years after a major fire, blueberries have been known to take over the blackened area.

The ubiquitous wild blueberry, also known as the huckleberry, is prized among wild-food gatherers.

Elderberries

Found along fencerows, roadsides and near old buildings, elderberry shrubs are 5 to 12 feet tall and sport upright stems that are green when young and turn a gray-brown when older. The saucer-shaped white flowers bloom in June or July. Campers must wait for late August when the rounded fruit turns a deep purple. For top taste, dry out the fruit in the sun on a blanket or newspaper.

Raspberries and Blackberries

More than 300 types grow in North America. Black raspberries are my favorite, and I find them along roadsides, trails, logging areas, the edges of woods and in open fields. The flowers are a green-white in spring, and the ripe fruit will easily slip off the stems from mid-July to mid-August. Black raspberries have long canes of 6 to 8 feet which often curve back to the ground, making impenetrable thickets. The red raspberry has similar flowers but smaller canes 2 to 5 feet). Blackberries, which also ripen in mid-summer, are found in open areas with plenty of sun.

Juneberries

Also called serviceberries or shadberries, the juneberry resembles large, purple-black blueberries growing on shrubs from knee-high to taller than a man. Five-petaled white flowers about an inch across bloom in early spring, and the fruit is ripe in late June to early July. The *canadensis* species is an Eastern fruit that grows as far west as Minnesota. The *florida* species ranges from Minnesota to the Pacific coast.

Mushrooms

Excellent as an accessory to fish, poultry and meat, mushrooms are a delicacy when mixed with salad greens or simply sautéed and eaten on their own merits. In my home state of Michigan grow more than 2,000 species, but because some mushrooms are poisonous, always consult an identification guide with color plates. An especially good one is Dr. Alexander Smith's *The Mushroom Hunter's Field Guide*.

People often react individually to mushrooms—beefsteak and false

Hard to find but wonderful to eat is the much-sought morel mushroom.

morel varieties, for example, can cause nausea in some eaters—and so never eat more than a small amount until you are certain of safety. As a general rule, the true morels are safe for consumption if not eaten raw.

Black Morels

Morchella augusticeps is the black morel although the color can vary from creamed coffee to brown-black. The ridged head is pitted with little hollows, not unlike corrugated cardboard, and may range in size from three-fourths inch to three inches long. Blacks are the first morels to appear, fruiting during a three- to five-week period beginning after warm rains in April and lasting through May.

White Morels

Morchella esculenta varies from a light tawny color to yellow-brown. Ridges of the pits are usually a light, almost-white color. The heads of both black and white morels are attached to their stalks at the base inside the cap. White morels vary in size from one to five inches.

Like most mushrooms, morels like rich, damp soil. Good places to look include the bottom of slopes where mineral soil meets organic soil, logging roads in wet areas, hardwood stands mixed with evergreens and a ground cover of bracken fern and trailing arbutus, and near dead elm trees.

From arrowhead to wintergreen, nature affords a bounty of edible plants, especially if picked young and eaten fresh. Again, positive identification is the key. Natural foods my family has enjoyed while camping and backpacking include:

Cattail Snack

The tubers of cattails have a mild cucumber taste and are excellent eaten raw or chopped up into a salad. Cattails grow in wet, marshy areas and are easily identified by their velvety heads.

Leek Soup

This member of the onion family grows in moist, shady soil, usually along creek bottoms and often near skunk cabbage and marsh marigolds. Pluck the bulb, then quarter and sauté as a side dish or mix in with salad greens. Leeks also make a wonderful flavoring to potato soup.

Fiddlehead ferns are tasty in a salad or as a side dish.

Fiddlehead Side Dish

The curly top part of a young fiddlehead fern (before the plant reaches a foot in height), is especially tasty when washed and then boiled until tender.

Sassafras or Birch Tea

When boiled in water, a handful of tiny broken twigs from the sassafras tree, easily identified by its triple-lobed leaves that resemble a mitten, make a mild tea which tastes like root beer. The young twigs from yellow or black birch are also popular as an aromatic tea.

Watercress Salad

This bright-green plant grows as a floating mat along seepages and stream bottoms throughout the country. Its pungent taste is excellent in salad, and it can be used to flavor soups, hor d'oeuvres and even sandwiches.

Sumac Lemonade

In late summer fill the bottom of a soup pan with red sumac berries, mash them down a bit, and add boiling water. After letting the mixture steep to full color, strain the liquid through cheesecloth to remove tiny hairs. Cool and enjoy your homemade drink.

CARE AND MAINTENANCE OF EQUIPMENT

"Pay me now or pay me later" was the popular line for a television ad touting the merits of preventive maintenance for cars. The same advice is true for campers and backpackers. Cleaning and maintaining equipment before you put it away assures that everything will be functional the next time you head outdoors. It's also the best way to realize the most value from your investment.

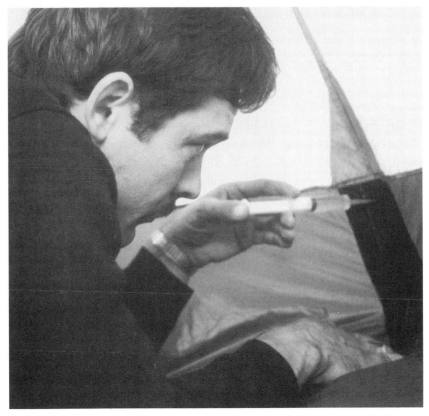

Periodically seam sealing your tent from the inside pays dividends when nights are stormy.

Tents. Check grommets, zippers, seams and screening, repairing as needed. Sweep out and wash the floor if dirty. Remove stains, bird droppings and other grime by washing with a mild detergent such as Murphy's Oil Soap. Thoroughly dry (hang on a line if necessary) the entire tent, including the bottom. Waterproof if necessary with Thompson's Water Seal or other product, and reseal the seams. Fold in a new pattern to spread the wear. Wrap in a canvas bag and store in a dry area, off the floor to prevent mildew. Replace frayed shock cords on tent poles, straighten bent stakes, sand and oil poles that section together.

Sleeping Bags and Pads. Air out and wash if necessary. Check condition of zippers and drawstrings, repairing or replacing as needed. Store in black, heavy-duty garbage bags and tie off to eliminate air.

Packs. If possible, turn inside out and shake out dirt. Wash with a sponge and mild detergent and air dry. Replace broken zippers, frayed shoulder straps, busted split rings, missing tie downs and clevis pins. Hang on wooden pegs in a cool, dry area.

Appliances. Drain fuel and clean appliance. Replace lantern mantles and generator if necessary. Oil pump leathers if so equipped.

Cookware. Wash, dry and store. Recure Dutch oven if needed.

Knives, Ax, Hatchet. Sharpen. then protect with a thin coating of oil. Check condition of sheath.

LEARNING CAMPCRAFT SKILLS

Many basic outdoor skills I learned as a Cub, Boy and Explorer Scout. Others, such as paddling a canoe, I discovered as a schoolboy trapper, which also taught me many things about conservation and Nature's mysterious web. Kids don't trap much anymore, but hunting, fishing and camping are still popular, and millions of people have gone through the Scouting and Campfire Girl programs. Perhaps more than anything else today, camping affords people not only the opportunity to appreciate the environment but also to learn outdoor skills.

Some campcraft know-how, such as building a fire, sharpening an ax, tying knots, and reading the weather have been handed down by our pioneer ancestors. Knowing how to perform these and other skills is still important because they make camping fun. They also can save lives.

Cutting Wood

Select dry, dead wood for building fires. Choose a dead tree that is still standing, and if the outside is wet, cut into the dry heart. Always use a sharp cutting edge. To drop a tree, estimate where it will fall, then cut a notch about one-third of the distance into the trunk on the same side the tree is leaning. Complete the cut by chopping a few inches higher; the tree will buckle along the original cut. Step quickly to the side as it falls to avoid a possible kickback.

Trim branches only when the tree is down and then cut with the slant of the branch, never against it. To cut cleanly across a branch or sapling for making tent stakes or poles, hold the sapling against another tree or a block of wood—never the ground or a rock. To cut through the tree, chop a wedge halfway on one side, then turn over the tree and complete the job.

Use a maul or single-bit ax to split chunks of firewood. Split only those logs that have been squared with a saw on both ends. Make sure the ax head is tightly secured, clear an area for twenty feet around you, and aim for cracks in the block you are about to split. If you use a saw, anchor the log in a sawhorse, easily made by lashing two pairs of logs in an X shape a few feet apart.

Building a Fire

Before striking a match, choose a designated spot (such as a fireplace ring) or find an area devoid of flammable material (dried grass, dead limbs that

The tepee fire is the simplest and most effective fire known.

overhang). Dig a pit for your fire, taking care to keep the topsoil chunk for replacement later. Remove any other burnable material within a few feet of the fire, and further protect the area by circling the fire with rocks.

Gather matches, tinder, kindling and bigger pieces of wood before you strike a match. Have a source of water nearby.

Good tinder materials include dried birchbark (peeled from downed trees), dead moss, newspaper, an old bird's nest, toothpick-thin wood shavings, pitch-impregnated pieces of evergreen wood, pine cones, mesquite branches, chunks of dead cholla cactus, and cotton balls dipped in petroleum jelly. You can make a fuzz stick, also called a prayer stick, by using a knife to peel the exterior of a soft, dry piece of wood without removing the shavings. Commercial jellied substances and tablets work fine, too, especially with magnesium striker tools. Never use gasoline or other liquid fuel to start a fire.

Gerber's Strike Force Fire Starter System relies on a spark generator rod, striker bar and small cube that ignites, even when floated in water. The cube burns for several minutes, long enough to get kindling going.

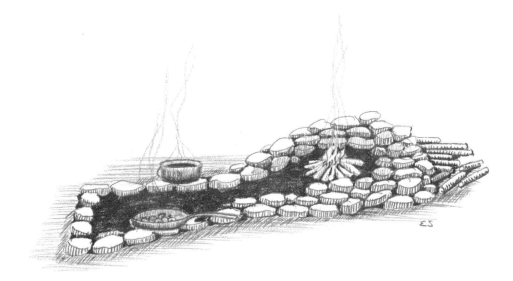

The keyhole fire allows food to be cooked and kept
warm at the same time.

Arrange the tinder in a small pile with plenty of openings for air. Add
dry kindling, starting with sticks of pencil size and finishing with those
the diameter of an index finger, in a tepee design. Once the kindling is
burning well, feed larger pieces of wood. Remember that smaller fires
are just as cheerful as raging bonfires and are easier to attend to and
clean up afterwards.

Once the tepee fire has burned down, it is fine for cooking (coals provide more even cooking heat than do licking flames). A narrow trench fire
works well for cooking, too, because heat is contained, any wind provides
a draft, and pots and pans can be supported by the trench sides.

When rocks are available, a better cooking fire is the keyhole design.
Arrange rocks in the shape of a keyhole, piling up the stones for two feet
or so at the top of the pattern. This wall of rock will reflect heat from the
fire, which should be built in the large opening. As coals appear, move
them to the narrow end of the keyhole where they will keep cooked
food hot. When rocks are not available use logs. Pounding the logs to
stakes in the ground at the top of the pattern and stacking a row of logs
atop each other will also reflect heat to some degree.

Sharpening an Edge

Always wear gloves when sharpening knives, hatchets and axes. I no longer sharpen knives with a whetstone, preferring instead to use commercially made V-shaped ceramic rods or guide-bar kits such as those made by Lansky Sharpeners and GATCO. They're simpler to use than whetstones and always produce a fine edge to my specialty knives used for filleting fish and skinning and boning game as well as the all-purpose Swiss Army Knife.

Chopping tools are another matter. You can sharpen them at home with a medium to fine flat mill file by securing the head in a table vice.

The proper method for sharpening an ax is to begin at the heel (bottom of the edge) and stroke toward the toe.

Finishing the edge with a whetstone will make the ax even sharper.

In the field, simply pound a wooden peg in the ground and brace the head against it. Secure the handle with your knee or a log. Using a 15- to 20-degree angle, begin filing at the heel (bottom) of the blade and stroke downward toward the toe (top), taking care to lift the file each time before starting over. Touching up your work with a whetstone will impart a razor-sharp edge.

Handling a Canoe

The more experienced paddler (we'll assume it is you) should be in the stern end. To get in safely, walk to the stern while bent over, toes turned in, holding onto the sides (gunwales). While you are doing this, your less-experienced partner should wedge the bow between his knees and hold the canoe steady until you are seated. Then he shoves off and steps in while you backpaddle into deeper water.

In calm water the canoe can be aimed into the water. After the bow person is comfortable, the stern paddler simply steps in and shoves off.

With your partner, practice paddling in calm water, and never stand in a canoe. If paddling alone, kneel just ahead of the back seat (usually in front of the rear thwart) to better position your weight and stabilize the canoe.

Learning the basic paddle strokes and canoe-handling techniques is easier than mastering bicycle riding. The bowman paddles on either side; watching him, the sternman paddles on the opposite side and is concerned with steering. Paddling techniques are a matter of learning two basic strokes and experimenting from there. The bow stroke (also called a cruising stroke or power stroke) is made by keeping the paddle as vertical as possible. The lower arm should be about even with the gunwale, the upper arm, with fingers curled over the paddle's shaft end, should be even with your eyes (paddle length dictates exact placement—the key is to be comfortable). Reach your arms forward, dip the paddle into the water, and propel it back by pushing forward with the upper hand. Keep the paddle on a near-vertical plane, and when it reaches your hip, lift it out and start over.

The stern stroke (also called a J stroke or fishhook stroke) is essentially the same, except the paddler feathers the paddle backward and outward as a rudder away from the canoe in the shape of a J. Making the J stroke just as the paddle reaches his hip, the stern man will be able to keep the canoe on course with a minimum of effort. Both paddlers should keep their backs straight. After a few minutes the partners will establish a harmonic rhythm.

Other tips:

• Load the canoe in a way to keep the bow slightly higher than the stern. Keep cargo as low as possible, and store in waterproof bags or a dry box. Cascades Designs, Voyageurs and Northwest River Supplies are a few of the many companies now making such watertight containers.

• When hauling camping gear, consider tying it to the gunwales or thwarts in the event of capsizing. Tying gear creates two problems, however: (1) you must untie everything to portage, (2) you can't easily shift the load when conditions change.

• When crossing a wide expanse of open water in a strong wind, quarter into the waves. Hug the lee side of islands and shore whenever possible. In an emergency, lash two canoes together and head for land.

The proper paddling technique for a solo canoeist: Kneel behind the center, put gear in front so the bow is slightly higher than the stern.

• Some canoes feature padded shoulder supports on the center thwart. You can also tie the paddles to gunwales and thwarts in a V-shape so that the shafts will rest on your shoulders. Cushion the paddles with a sweatshirt or hot pads used for cooking.

• Don't run unfamiliar rapids without first beaching the canoe and scouting. "Read" the stream to determine where submerged obstacles are and plan how you will negotiate them. Lining the canoe through rapids with the help of ropes attached to bow and stern is often an option. So is the portage.

Changing a Lantern Mantle

Remove the globe and clean away the broken mantle and its tie string. Use your fingers to open the new mantle as wide and round as possible, then use a simple knot to secure the strings furnished with the new mantle to the fuel mount. Trim pieces of string longer than a quarter-inch (some newer mantles do not require tying—they simple fit over the fuel mount like a sock).

Open the fuel tank cap to release any pressure. Wait a minute and then light the new mantle with a match, allowing it to completely burn to a gray-white ash. Do this task outdoors because the burning process smells and creates a good deal of smoke. Replace the globe. Wait five minutes after the mantle has ceased to smoke, then light the lantern according to printed directions.

Tying Knots

Learning (or relearning) the ropes by practice tying a few important knots is worth any camper's time and effort. Tents and cooking shacks will remain erect in the strongest wind. Your canoe will stay atop the car roof the next time a semi truck-trailer goes roaring by. Knot knowledge is critical for dozens of uses from securing clotheslines to clearing a two-track of downed timber. Boat anchors, fish stringers and dock lines all require the use of purposeful, strong knots. Backpackers use them for securing food out of a bear's reach. Good knots can save a mountain climber's life.

Bowline. The knot of a hundred uses, the bowline may be the most important of all to learn. Easy to tie and untie, it gains strength as it is tightened and is especially useful for securing a loop around logs, trees or other objects. The bowline is the ideal knot for towing heavy things such as trees and even cars in an emergency.

Clove Hitch. Another simple knot for tying a rope to a tree, pole or stake, the clove hitch amounts to a pair of loops joined together so the knot becomes tighter when pulled in either direction. Making the hitch in the middle of a long rope frees up both ends for other knots and other uses.

Horse Hitch. A more complicated knot that serves a specialized purpose, the horse hitch holds a pack animal in place, yet is easily undone in an emergency. After tying the hitch, the key is to pass the running end of the rope through a big open loop. Not only does this make the knot more secure, but when removing the running end from the loop and jerking, the hitch loosens immediately.

Square Knot. Easily confused with the easy-to-slip granny knot, the square knot (also called a reef knot) holds forever. To tie it correctly, remember to loop under (and not over) with the second or upper knot. Looping this knot over results in the near-worthless granny. The square knot is great for joining two ropes or for tying together the ends of a single rope. Like the bowline, it's a cinch to untie.

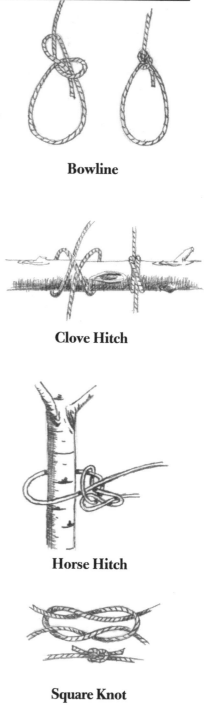

Bowline

Clove Hitch

Horse Hitch

Square Knot

Half-hitch. Perhaps the simplest of all knots to tie, the half-hitch is merely the first half of a shoelace knot turned sideways. Two or three consecutive half-hitches make a fairly strong knot, but they are a nuisance to untie.

Slip Knot. Half-hitches are helpful for securing the slip knot, which is useful for adjusting rope guys on a tent until the correct tension is achieved. Adding half-hitches finishes the job.

Timber Hitch. Similar to the bowline, the timber hitch is handy for dragging heavy objects and for securing rope to ridgepoles and tree limbs. The knot is a simple half-hitch with the running end turned back on itself.

Guy-line Hitch. Another knot for this purpose is the guy-line hitch, which is simply a pair of overhand knots with the rope passing through the upper one. The lower knot then slides to give or take up slack.

Taut-line Hitch. Yet another good knot for tightening and securing tent ropes is the taut-line hitch. It's actually a running loop, which you can alter easily, but the timber or clove hitch will perform equally well and is easier to tie.

Double Sheet Bend. Have you ever experienced the need to tie two ropes of different diameter together? This task is performed easily with the double sheet bend. Always make the loop with the bigger rope, and use the thinner diameter rope to make the bends around it. Be sure to make two turns with the smaller

Half-hitch

Slip Knot

Timber Hitch

Guy-line Hitch

Taut-line Hitch

Double Sheet Bend

rope. It takes only another second and makes the knot doubly strong.

Diamond Hitch. Also called the government hitch, this knot and various versions of it are widely used by wranglers securing loads of equipment to horses and other pack animals.

Carrick Bend. The carrick bend is used to secure heavy loads or tow heavy objects. It won't bind and is easy to undo.

Figure-eight Knot. Ropes that fray on the ends or unbraid can be a nuisance. If the cord is made from synthetic material such as nylon, melt the ends with a match and then allow to cool. Wrapping the last few inches with duct tape or electrician's tape will stop unraveling, too, at least temporarily. A better way to eliminate this problem is with the figure-eight knot.

Whipping. Another trick to end unraveling is called whipping. Use a strong thread or thin twine to secure rope ends and then dip them in epoxy or an all-purpose glue. Or seal with flame.

Purifying Water

Never assume that water is safe to drink unless it has passed government inspection, a regular requirement at organized campgrounds. In the backcountry, and even in settled areas, hikers and backpackers can get into serious trouble by drinking unsafe water. The best insurance against con-

Diamond Hitch

Carrick Bend

Figure-eight Knot

Whipping

tracting *Giardia lamblia* or other microorganism is to carry your own water from home. Plan on drinking at least two quarts per day, and four quarts daily if you will be exercising strenuously and the weather is warm.

A pair of one-liter Nalgene bottles with screw caps is typical cargo for backpackers, meaning they'll have to find a source of water on overnight trips. If you must take water from the environment, try to collect it from springs or stream headwaters where the water is coldest and animals are less likely to frequent. Avoid stagnant ponds or pools. If a lake is your only source, collect from the middle.

Boiling water for two minutes should kill any micro-organisms; in fact, giardiasis perishes by the time water reaches its boiling point. A second method is to treat the water with Halozene or iodine tablets or drops (household bleach won't kill all the potential bugs). To mitigate the chemical taste, remove the cap for an hour and allow the container to breath.

Filtering with an approved system that captures particles to 1 micron or less is the modern way to extract potable water. Some filters, like the PentaPure Travel Cup, use an iodinated resin to kill bacteria too small to be caught by filtration. Here's how it works: contaminants, which are negatively charged, are drawn to the positively charged resin. Upon contact, the resin releases enough iodine to kill the contaminants.

Reading the Weather

Bad weather ruins more camping and backpacking trips than equipment malfunction, scheduling errors and incompatible partners combined. No one can beat Nature at her own weather game, but being able to forecast problems before they occur and then taking proper precautions can help smooth any outdoor experience.

Wind is responsible for weather changes, and so it makes sense to be attuned to the breezes, the directions from which they blow, and the resulting changes in cloud patterns. Scattered high cirrus clouds with their "mare's tails" mean a fair-weather system. Cumulus clouds are the white, cottony puffs of mid-height that usually spell good weather, too, except when their bottoms turn gray from moisture gathering. Then it will rain soon. Low, nimbus clouds mean it will rain soon if it hasn't already started. Those that are heavy and gray and blot out the sun are called nimbostratus clouds and could portend bad weather for days on end.

Some campers and backpackers like to carry a pocket barometer. Using the baseline reference of 29.92 inches of mercury at sea level, and factoring in the roughly one inch of gain for every thousand feet of altitude, they keep an eye on the instrument for the slightest change.

A rising barometer means a high-pressure system, which translates to clearing skies and favorable weather. A falling barometer means a low-pressure system with bad weather—usually in the form of rain—on its way.

The more time you spend outdoors, the more capable you will grow at predicting the weather. Long before AccuWeather radar forecasting systems, people depended on folklore and oral tradition to figure out what the weather would do. There is still a lot of truth to the old sayings, which are fun to learn:

Dry day or wet day? About an hour after this photograph was taken, it began to rain. Signs indicated a gathering of nimbus clouds and a falling barometer.

Evening fog will not burn soon;
Morning fog will burn before noon.

There's a reason for that, as there is with all weather maxims. As both
the sun and morning thermals rise, fog will burn off. Because evening
air settles, an oncoming fog will usually last all night.

Red sky at morning, sailors take warning;
Red sky at night, sailors delight.

Apparently a weather change is brewing, but it is at least twelve hours
away. A little twist on that favorite of the farmer's almanacs goes like this:

**An old saying is that mountains make their own weather. It is proba-
bly snowing in Alaska's Brooks Range in the background. Later on
this August day, it began to snow here.**

> Evening red and morning grey,
> Speed the traveler on his way.
> Evening grey and morning red
> Bring down rain upon his head.

Better make sure that sunset is red, though, and not yellow because,

> Yellow streaks in sunset sky,
> Wind and day-long rain is nigh.

Ever notice how fierce rainstorms don't usually last too long? That's because,

> The sharper the blast, the sooner it's past.

Or how rain is at best intermittent when the day is bright? Of course:

> A sunshiny shower won't last half an hour.

If you're a pessimist, this little saying will make your day:

> The south wind brings wet weather;
> The north wind, wet and cold together;
> The west wind always brings us rain.
> The east wind blows it back again.

Campers pay special heed to this one:

> East-floating smoke is bad;
> West-floating smoke is good.

The logic of that pithy saying is that a west wind (which chases smoke to the east) usually brings rain. On the other hand, an easterly wind heralds good weather.

> When dew is on the morning grass,
> Rain will not come to pass.

Morning dew follows clear nights. Conversely, if there is no dew on the grass by the middle of the night, chances are it will rain before morning.

And speaking of rain,

> Rain before seven, quit by eleven.

Before dousing the campfire and turning in, you might as well check out the moon:

Clear moon, frost soon.

Clear moons occur more often in fall because there are fewer clouds to hold in the earth's heat.

Pale moon doth rain, red moon doth blow.
White moon doth neither rain nor snow.

For centuries the moon has looked different to poets, astronomers and weather-watchers, but that is mostly due to atmospheric clarity or the lack of it.

Spend enough time outdoors, and you will no doubt come up with your own guide to the weather. I have learned, for example, that aspen leaves bellying up in a silver shimmer almost always mean a storm is coming fast. Campfire smoke that doesn't wander but rather departs straight up means a high-pressure system. When smoke lies low in the woods, though, don't forget to pack a raincoat.

Finding Your Way

Getting lost—really lost and not just turned around—is a frightening, humiliating experience. Yet it is a rite of passage that every woods-wise outdoorsman has experienced, whether or not he admits it. The alternative, though, is never learning to orientate yourself and you know what that means: a lifetime of camping in organized campgrounds, of never pitching a tent on some top-of-the-mountain stream, of never canoeing onto a good bass lake when the stars come out.

So, if you have yet to experience finding your way out of the woods, get lost—on purpose—but in a controlled situation. Find a wooded area, for example, that is bounded by mile-section roads so that no matter how turned around you become, you will find the way out. The experience will teach you to use a compass correctly and how to read a map. Next time outdoors you will remember to take a bearing and to look over your shoulder in order to recall landmarks later when you retrace your steps. You will become more familiar with the woods, too, and in the event that you must spend a night outdoors, you'll be better equipped to handle it.

Getting lost can be a frightening, humiliating experience, but it can also teach you how to use a compass.

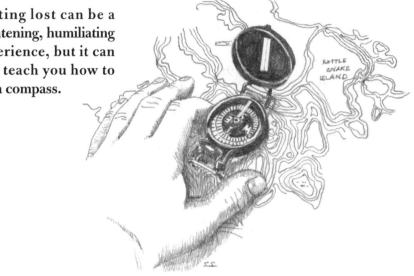

The first rule of being lost is not to panic. Take several deep breaths and get control of yourself. Unless you're in the Arctic or deep in some Amazon jungle, you can't be more than a few hours from help. Sit down (standing, you're more inclined to run in blind fear) and assess the situation, calmly. Eat a candy bar. Relax. Go over the travel route in your mind. Now, how far is it from that last landmark?

Once you've settled down, retrace your line of travel as you remember it. If you have a compass and took a bearing before departing, walk back in the opposite direction until you come out to familiar surroundings. Always believe your compass. The top of the map in your pocket will probably be north. Not sure? By squinting at the sun or looking at the shadow from a twig held across your palm (assuming there is no sun), you should be able to determine east and west.

If there is sun, point the hour hand on your watch directly at it. Halfway to 12 o'clock is south; north, obviously is the opposite direction. If the night is clear you can find north by locating the North Star. It lies in the same line as the two stars that form the outside of the cup on the Big Dipper.

If you can't figure out directions and are certain you're lost, then get as comfortable as possible and stay put until help arrives.

The shortest distance between two points is not always a straight line when one has lakes and mountains to negotiate. Knowing how you got into the woods is the best way to knowing the way out, and it takes on added importance when you have a canoe or heavy pack on your back.

Topographic Map

A good compass and reliable map are valuable tools only if you know how to use them. Satellite imaging and infra-red photography have provided campers and hikers with new and exciting maps that are actual photographs, many of which are overlaid with a scale and identification.

Topographic maps, though, are the most popular because they contain a wealth of information, as any backpacker or wilderness canoeist will attest. Topo maps give elevations in contours of brown print, but they also point out rivers and lakes (blue), key roads (red), man-made objects such as dams and buildings (black) and vegetation (green). Popular scales are 1 inch to 250,000 inches (1:250,000), or 1 inch equals 4 miles; 1:62,500 or 1 inch equals 1 mile; and 1:24,000 or 1 inch equals 2,000 feet. Larger and smaller scale topo maps are also available.

Using a Compass

The difference between true north and magnetic north (the direction a compass actually points) is called declination. This declination may vary by as much as 20 degrees west for someone living in Maine to as much as 30 degrees east for a resident of Alaska. To allow pinpoint map compass readings, all topo maps explain declination with a simple diagram.

Each topo map allows you, then, to use an orienteering or "map" compass (one containing a travel arrow, 360-degree gradation and an inch ruler—don't waste your money on cheaper compasses that have simply N, E, S and W imprinted on them). With a good map compass, you can determine exact distances between locations and chart an accurate course. To use correctly: (1) point the travel arrow at a landmark; (2) turn the rotating dial until the magnetic arrow (usually red in color) lines up with the travel arrow; (3) read the bearing in degrees.

To illustrate: Let's assume your travel course is north/northeast at 40 degrees (40 degrees east of north). To find the way back, add 180 degrees (half of a circle). In this example, the way out then is 220 degrees south/southwest. When walking in either direction, pick out a landmark, such as a big pine tree, walk to that spot, check your bearing and pick out additional landmarks, one at a time, until you reach your destination. With a little practice, you should be able to find your way.

A good place to practice orienteering is on a golf course where the various greens and their flags serve as landmarks. A well-equipped sporting goods outlet will have a good selection of compasses as well as books and videos. The latest development in orienteering taps into the Global Positioning System (GPS) that depends on satellites designed primarily for the nation's defense. Hand-held GPS receivers like the Magellan NAV 5000 weigh mere ounces yet allow boaters, backpackers, campers, hunters and fishermen to use satellite data to figure out current location, altitude and speed. Once you have a position fix, information can be computed in less than a minute and is updated every second. Think of a GPS unit as an electronic compass that constantly records your speed and direction as you walk. Although expensive (about $1,000 at this writing), price points are coming down as more manufacturers enter the market.

Building an Emergency Shelter

If you have to spend a night outdoors and have no tent or sleeping gear, the key is to stay warm and dry. A space blanket, which weighs mere ounces and tucks into a shirt pocket or backpack, can help you through the night, and it makes an excellent rescue reflector to hang from a tree the next day.

If you have matches and can find dry wood, build two fires and sleep between them.

A tarp or piece of heavy-duty plastic can provide a lean-to shelter against the wind and will reflect heat from your campfire. Simply tie a rope between two trees and hang the tarp over it, then stake out the bottom end at a 45-degree angle to the ground. Use clothespins or heavy-duty paper binder clips to secure the tarp edge to the rope. If the tarp is long enough, fold some of it back to make a ground cover.

The tarp can also provide a canopy in the event of rain. Lay the covering across the rope like you would a sheet on a clothesline. Lifting each of the four corners, hold a small, smooth rock under the material, push the material up (like inserting your hand in your pocket), and use a six-foot-long piece of rope to tie a knot under each fabric-covered rock. The four rock ties provide anchor points for staking the four ropes to the ground.

You can also make a temporary shelter without benefit of tools or rope material. While camping with native fishing guides in the jungles of Venezuela, I noticed they could erect a comfortable, rain-tight sleeping shelter in only a couple of hours by using saplings and palm leaves, lashing the roof and walls together with tough vines. The shelter even featured an off-the-ground bed away from scorpions and spiders.

The simplest shelter is made by breaking down a thick evergreen tree at a 45-degree angle about four or five feet off the ground and then crawling under the boughs for protection. To make a lean-to, wedge a ridge pole into tree forks a few feet apart and an equal distance above the ground. Slant several more poles along one side of the ridge pole, then thatch that side with evergreen boughs, starting from the bottom and working toward the top.

Removing a Fishhook

A fishhook embedded in a dangerous area like the eye should be treated by an emergency-room doctor as quickly as possible. Superficial hookings in nonthreatening areas can usually be removed with a minimum amount of pain. Simply back the hook out and treat the wound with an antiseptic, then cover with a Band-Aid if necessary. If the victim has had a recent tetanus shot, that's the end of the problem.

A deeply embedded fishhook (past the barb) will be painful to remove by either one of two approved methods. The size of the hook and how deep it is buried should dictate which procedure is best. To back the hook out, loop strong monofilament line around what remains

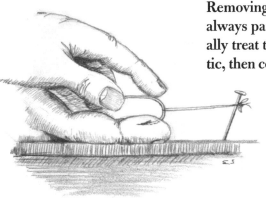

Removing an embedded fish hook is always painful. After removal, liberally treat the wound with an antiseptic, then cover with a bandage.

of the hook bend, press down on the shank, and give a hard jerk. If no one is available to pull the hook out, tie the monofilament to a nail or tree and perform the disagreeable task yourself.

An often better way and one that creates less damage to the flesh is to push the hook forward so that the barb protrudes. Cut it off and then back the now barbless hook out.

Riding a Horse

Campers inexperienced around horses needn't be afraid of them but should exercise a healthy respect and a commonsense dose of caution. Here are some tips:

• Approach a strange horse where it can see you. If you must walk up from behind, alert the animal by saying its name in a calm voice.

• Unless it's necessary, don't mount in a confined area; if you're thrown, you could be injured.

• Always mount from the animal's left side. Put the ball of your left foot in the stirrup, grasp the mane in your left hand and the saddlehorn in your right. Mount in one quick, smooth motion.

• Wear hard-soled shoes, preferably with a heel. Not only will such footwear give you a better "bite" in the stirrup, but you will protect your toes against an errant step by the horse.

• Hold the reins in your left hand. Keep your right hand free and loose.

• Remember that reins are used for control—much like power steering on a car. A horse's mouth is as sensitive to the bit as a steering suspension is to the road. Don't jerk the reins except to regain control over a spooked horse. Even then, don't overly muscle the animal, and speak softly to it in a calm and consistent tone.

• Don't let reins droop over a horse's head where he could step on them.

• Always ride with the balls of your feet in the stirrup to aid in quick dismounting. Use your knees as shock absorbers.

• Learn to anticipate a horse's moves before he makes them. Watch the animal's eyes and especially its ears for telltale signs of mischief and fear.

• Learn to tie the horse hitch. It's the most important knot to know. The diamond hitch, explained and illustrated under knots, is useful for packing gear.

• Hitching, saddling and cinching can be taught to any greenhorn by a patient teacher. Knowing how to do these and other simple but necessary tasks will help you relax around your mount and better understand its behavior.

Loading and Leading a Pack Animal

Packing a horse the right way requires some experience. Food and camping equipment like stoves and lanterns should be protected in pack boxes. Unbreakable gear like sleeping bags, pads and tents can be arranged in pack sacks or panniers with rope loops, which can then be slung over the wooden cross braces of the no-stirrup sawbuck pack saddles.

Gear can also be wrapped in canvas mantas and tied securely, then slung over the saddle. Foam sleeping mats and empty burlap grain bags help to cushion a fragile or noisy load, such as rattling cookware that could spook a pack animal. Put all clothing in a duffel bag. Fishing rods should be encased in rigid-walled tube containers.

Pack the string according to when you'll need the gear. For trail clear-

An animal whose pack weight is unevenly distributed, even by a few pounds, may experience trouble keeping its balance in situations like crossing a swift river.

ing, the saw and ax should go on the lead animal, along with the mess tent and kitchen supplies. Sleeping tents are next, followed by personal gear, then the tack tent and food for the horses. Always separate food from lantern and stove fuel, and sheath the sharp edges of cutting tools.

The weight must be evenly distributed—50 to 100 pounds to each side of the animal depending on its size and strength—within 3 pounds left and right. An experienced packer can determine weight by simply lifting gear. Those of us who cannot should suspend a spring scale with a hook from a tree limb.

Some pack horses in particular tend to be a bit wild, which is why they're not used as ride animals. Gregarious by nature, horses establish a pecking order. If there's a stallion in the group (and there shouldn't be if you've hired an outfitter) he'll be the ringleader. To avoid a rodeo on the trail, don't string together horses that are clearly hostile to each other. Let the toughest wrangler deal with any troublesome horses.

You can lead a pack animal by carrying its halter in your right hand or looping it once around your saddlehorn (never tie it tightly) so you can drop the rope quickly in case of a fall or brouhaha. Occasionally packers will tie a halter to the tail of the animal in front, but most loop halters over saddle pommels. In rough country a few use baling twine or other light rope at the end of the halter for a quick breakaway if trouble occurs.

100 TIPS AND TECHNIQUES

Serious campers and backpackers are forever finding new ways to be comfortable and safe in the outdoors. In addition to the tips and techniques sprinkled throughout this book, what follows are 100 additional ways to save money, make maximum use of equipment, and have more fun. If you're on a tight budget, also refer to the last section for Cost-Buster Camping ideas.

1. Make campground charcoal at home by adding green hardwood branches or saplings one to two inches thick and a foot long to your barbecue grill when you are finished cooking for the day. Allow just enough air flow through the grill to "cook" the wood into charcoal.

2. Another charcoal tip: Wash and dry a half-gallon milk carton. Add briquets and a little tinder. Besides not having to handle the dirty charcoal, you can make a good fire by simply lighting the waxy milk container.

3. Punching holes in the ends of tin cans, then sliding them halfway up table legs will keep critters from crawling atop the table.

4. To make diesel sticks for fire starting, soak dry kindling in a pail of diesel fuel. Much like expensive "fat wood," the kindling will soak up the fuel and will burn steadily—even in the rain—to help you build that next fire. Carry the diesel sticks in a Zip-Loc or other airtight bag.

5. Silicone spray will temporarily waterproof a backpack, hat, shoes and other items you don't want to get wet.

6. Coat hangers make ideal pot grabbers. A piece of sturdy wire will also suffice.

7. Rubbing soap on a stuck zipper on a pack or sleeping bag will sometimes free it up until you can properly repair it. Silicone will also do the job temporarily.

8. To prevent blowback when heating a wall tent with a woodburning stove, make sure the stovepipe is above the ridge line of the tent.

9. Never leave an ax or hatchet buried upright in a block of wood where someone could trip and injure himself. For safety's sake, sheath the ax and store it in your vehicle or tent. If you must secure it in a log, turn the log over.

10. To find water, dig in the lowest spot around, such as dried river beds and depressions between hills. To collect water, even from the desert, make a solar still by digging a hole three feet wide and two feet deep. Place a collection container in the middle of the hole, and spread a piece of thin polyethlene over the hole. Secure the plastic around the hole perimeter with excavated dirt, then place a small rock in the center of the plastic. Evaporated moisture will hit the sheet, condense, and run back into the container. A few handfuls of grass or green leaves in the hole will increase the amount of water collected.

11. Wrapping aluminum foil around pots and pans precludes your having to scrub otherwise-blackened cookware. Soaping the cookware before using it serves the same purpose. On the other hand, know that blackened cookware heats faster and saves fuel.

12. An empty one- or two-gallon fuel can turns into a makeshift stove

The best army surplus wall tents are those formerly used as cook tents. Subjected to smoke and cooking fumes, the canvas will be better preserved and last longer.

if you cut away the top half, punch holes in the sides, build a small fire, and tip the can over so you can cook on the flat bottom. Skewering a couple of metal rods through the upper portion turns the can into a simple oven, too.

13. Toss a couple of giant-size paper-clip binders into your backpack. They'll come in handy for pinching a torn tent flap or mosquito netting, double as a simple C clamp, can hold a stove windscreen in place, and have a dozen other uses on the trail. Alligator clamps are also useful for these and other purposes.

14. A 30-foot-long piece of nylon parachute cord takes up little space and has a multitude of uses, including fishing line, shoelaces, clothesline and for securing a food cache above ground.

15. To cut down on pack weight, choose utensils that can do double duty. A slotted spoon, for example, can serve as a colander; a Sierra cup doubles as a soup ladle.

This homemade wooden pantry doubles to organize food and kitchen gear in the tent and protect it during transit.

16. Wooden hinged boxes for storing camping gear are handy to use as tables, cutting boards, seats and work areas.

17. Because oxygen levels are lower and barometic pressure is less (about one inch per 900 feet) at high altitudes, liquids take considerably longer to boil.

18. A couple of drops of lemon or lime juice will wake up flat-tasting water. Bits of peel from these fruits or an orange also work.

19. A self-inflating foam pad will last longer if you store it open with the valve loosened in a cool, dry place.

20. Reversing one battery in your flashlight safeguards against accidental discharge of power when you don't need it.

21. Lithium and alkaline batteries greatly outlast the dry-cell type.

22. A lightweight red bandana can be used for many purposes: protection from the sun, a sieve for straining water, a temporary tourniquet or first-aid wrap, a signal for help. If bugs are bad, spray it with insect repellent and wear it around your neck.

23. Clean plates and cookware with scour rush, also called horseweeds, that grows in wet areas and is easily identified by its segmented green stems.

24. Spare clevis pins secured to the zippers on an external-frame pack make wonderful pull tabs and are readily available to mend a broken pack.

25. Pick up a clothes bar from a trailer supply outlet (or make a clothes bar from a one-inch-diameter wooden dowel) and hang it in your truck topper or van. You can eliminate the need for suitcases, and the clothing can be used as temporary curtains over windows for privacy.

26. A few drops of Seam-Sealer added to a mattress pad will keep your sleeping bag from sliding off.

27. Sleeping with a water bottle at night gives you something to sip on in dry weather. Adding hot water will aid in warming your sleeping bag before turning in.

28. Thoroughly break in boots before hitting the trail. Nothing is worse than blistered feet when you have miles to go.

29. Rubber bands placed around your pants cuffs will cut down on attacks from mosquitoes and other biting insects.

30. A plastic ground cloth keeps the bottom of your tent floor clean and helps protect it from rough ground and water. Cut the ground cloth just big enough to fit inside the tent floor. If you extend it beyond the tent floor, it will collect water.

31. Seal all stitched seams on your tent by applying a brand-name product, such as Seam-Sealer, to the uncoated (inside) of the fabric. Water-repellent chemicals, which are often factory-applied to the outside, normally won't accept the seal.

32. Two different sizes of empty shotshells—inserted one into the other—make an ideal match container. To waterproof, add duct tape or melt paraffin around the seal.

33. Always pack biodegradable soap when backpacking and camping away from commercial washrooms.

34. To quiet a canoe, slit a section of old rubber garden hose and fit it over the gunwale at the paddling positions.

35. Shove anything breakable into the middle of your sleeping bag, whether rolled or in a stuff sack. A sleeping bag will also act as a temporary cooler.

36. Use a safety pin to secure a sock to the tent flap. Drop a flashlight into the sock so everyone knows where it is when they need it.

37. A piece of wire mesh screen over a wood-burning stovepipe makes a good spark arrestor. Burn a quick, hot fire occasionally to

A little imagination goes a long way toward making camp comfortable, especially if you forget items like potholders.

remove creosote buildup. Sagebrush, dried cholla cactus, mesquite and split dry pine are good fuels. Newspapers (with the exception of colored pages) will also do the job.

38. A Frisbee has many uses in camp. Besides providing an opportunity to unwind after a day of travel, the Frisbee can double as a plate or drinking cup, a container for berries and mushrooms, or as a wash basin.

39. To make a potgrabber or a potholder for cooking over an open fire, cut a green stick with a branch angling down. Hang the stick from its natural notch on the crane pole or tripod over your fire. Cutting notches an inch apart in the lower portion of the stick allows you to raise or lower the pot. The same creation will work to suspend a lantern from a branch if you have no wire or nails.

40. When sleeping in extreme cold, you can make a Vapor Barrier Liner by wearing a plastic garbage bag over your long underwear. Another thought is to wear your raincoat to bed. To protect extremities, wear empty sandwich bags or bread sacks over hands and feet.

41. In a destination camp without toilet facilities, dig a latrine between two trees four feet apart. To make a seat, lash two poles parallel to each other at sitting height to the trees. Lashing a third pole 18 inches higher serves as a back rest. Cover the spool of toilet paper with a tin can. Gradually fill in the hole with dirt after each use.

42. Strapping fishing rods under the gunwale of a canoe will save space and protect the rods from damage by streamside branches and carelessly-placed feet.

43. If you need earplugs, tear a couple of small pieces of foam from the corner of your sleeping pad.

44. To make a pillow, push extra clothing into an empty stuff sack.

45. A candle fire will burn hot enough to boil water if there is no wind. Put a tin can over the candle with a rock or two at the bottom for draft. A circle of stones will support a pot.

46. A heavy woolen sock makes a good hotpad if you forgot to bring one. Wear two socks on the same hand for extra protection.

47. Carry your map, notepad and pencil (you'll never run out of ink with a pencil) in a Ziploc bag.

48. A woman traveling and camping alone can prevent unwanted visitors by placing a large pair of men's boots outside her tent flap.

49. Dry boots are one of camping's greatest pleasures, and they are an absolute necessity for the long-distance backpacker. Placing them upside down on a warm rock will help dry the interiors, even after the sun has disappeared. Pack electric boot dryers in your vehicle in the event the next campground has electricity.

50. To keep a fuel canister warm in cold weather, put it in your sleeping bag until it heats up, then wrap it in a piece of foam. A beverage can insulating sock works great. If the sock is too small, merge a pair by slitting the sides and joining with a stout rubber band.

51. Park your canoe, boat, raft or kayak in a sheltered cove. If possible drag it to shore; if not, tie a rope around a tree and secure it to the craft.

52. Bears don't want a confrontation with humans anymore than campers want to meet bruins on the trail. The key is to let the bear know you're around before you meet accidentally. Good bear scares include a whistle on a lanyard, a small sheep's bell attached to your pack, your drinking cup, or a tin can with a few pebbles for rattling.

53. An old plastic shower curtain makes a fine ground cloth for your tent. If necessary, cut it to be no larger than the tent floor. Recycle the self-closing curtain rings, too—they come in handy as giant safety pins.

54. A wide-mouth, clear-plastic Nalgene bottle is best for drinking water because it is easy to keep clean and refill. Screw-type caps won't spill.

55. Although denim jeans are fashionable and comfortable, they take a long time to dry when wet. You're better off wearing lightweight wash-and-wear pants.

56. Eat the heaviest food in your pack first.

57. A small container of medicated talcum powder affords tremendous relief for tired, sore feet. It will also mask foot odor in the confines of a small tent.

58. Protecting your cookstove against wind can stretch fuel rations double or even triple. Nearly anything will do: piece of cardboard, dining place mat, even your sleeping pad in a pinch but don't get it too close to the flame.

59. The fastest way to dry out a sleeping bag is to drape it over a big rock in the direct sun.

60. To make a simple lantern, place a candle in a shallow tin can (a tuna can works well). A discarded Nalgene water bottle is fine, too, if you use a wide-mouth variety and are careful not to let the candle flame too near the plastic.

61. A canvas tarp across the roof of a wall tent acts as an excellent rain fly, plus it will hold heat better in winter.

62. Your tent can become a clothes dryer for wet clothes, especially on hot, sunny days. Rig a clothesline inside, hang the wet garments, and open both ends for ventilation.

63. A piece of carpet remnant makes a decent sleeping pad at little or no cost.

64. A fabric shoe organizer—the kind many women suspend in their closets—has unlimited storage uses around camp. Personal toiletry items, kitchen spices, small tools and other gear that is easily lost or misplaced can be dropped into the many pockets for safekeeping.

65. Every year campers toss away millions of small propane cylinders. Replenish them to three-fourths full from bulk propane tanks for about 25 cents each with a slick adaptor called the MacCoupler, available from K-M Products, 110 Tamara, Kalkaska, MI 49646 (616-258-9034). Bulk tanks on travel trailers, motor homes and patio barbecue grills are ideal sources of propane. Federal law prohibits the resale of cylinders not approved for refilling, but the pressure is too low for danger from explosion, and there is no law forbidding their personal use.

66. Pin a string to a small tent leak in the ceiling and run the string to the floor away from the sleeper's face. Water will run down the string.

67. Banking the wall tent with straw helps keep drafts and mosquitoes out and holds heat in. If the tent does not come with a perimeter sod cloth, sew a three-foot-wide flap all around. Tucking the sod flap inside will also cut down on drafts.

68. To fashion a makeshift floor for your tent, lash together a number of same-size poles (stripped of branches) about five inches in diameter and nail rough-sawn lumber over them.

69. A heavy piece of rope will work as a tent ridgepole if a proper pole can't be found or cutting one is illegal.

70. If your hiking boots don't have a trash collar and you are walking in sand, woods with thick undergrowth, the desert, or other places where debris finds its way into your footwear, slap on a pair of snow gaiters for protection.

71. Scrap carpeting in a pickup truck makes a soft, comfortable bed-liner, stops material from sliding around, and helps soundproof road noise. The carpeting is easily lifted out for cleaning.

Backpackers often carry a signal mirror in the event of emergency.

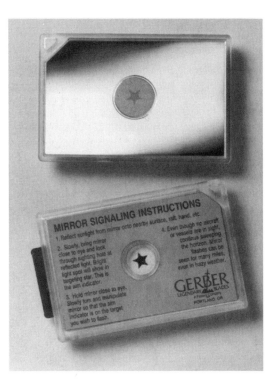

72. Adding Styrofoam sponsons to the gunwales of an aluminum canoe will add stability and reduce noise.

73. A second pair of insoles for hiking boots adds little weight to your pack and gives welcome relief to your feet. Woven fabric material stays cooler than foam rubber.

74. Forget a mirror and there isn't one in the restroom? Use the side-mount mirror on your vehicle

75. To make an RV more affordable, share the cost among friends. Consider renting out your RV or ask friends to at least pay the insurance premium. You might also reverse the idea and offer to rent or pay the insurance on a friend's unit in exchange for borrowing privileges.

76. When camping in cold weather, getting rid of moisture inside your tent is a must. Think of your tent as a chimney: Venting the bottom brings in cold air to replace warm, moisture-laden air that passes through a top vent.

77. The same practice applies to clothing. Opening the collar of your shirt and pulling the tails from your pants allows cold air to enter the bottom and exit the top.

78. A small piece of medium-grade sandpaper has many trail and camp uses such as smoothing the joints of a tent pole for a better connection, roughing up fabric for a repair patch, and striking a match.

79. When trailering a boat, you can store camping gear in the craft itself. Place heavy items ahead of the rear axle, and cover everything with a cover to prevent theft.

80. Carry a 3-inch-long piece of copper tubing to splice a broken aluminum or fiberglass backpacking tent pole. Be sure to get tubing whose inside diameter is slightly larger that the outside diameter of the pole.

81. Light a fire on the upwind side so that flames can spread throughout. Erect your tent on the upwind side, too.

82. When traveling with a pet, check your homeowner's insurance policy to make certain it protects you against liability. If your dog injures another through fighting or if it bites someone, you will likely be held responsible.

83. Many campers and backpackers rely on a small, windproof cigarette lighter for firing stoves and lanterns. You should always pack waterproof, strike-anywhere matches in event of emergency.

84. Adding rope hooks and bungee cords to the sidewalls of your van or pickup truck gives you a vertical place to secure backpacks and other gear.

85. If you take along your dog on the trail, let him carry his own food, water and bowl. At least two companies, Caribou Mountaineering and Granite Gear, make dog packs that ride like saddlebags and secure underneath the animal.

86. Dental floss turns into strong sewing thread for repairing a tent or backpack on the trail.

87. A few feet of aluminum foil is handy for cooking fish, cobbed corn and potatoes. Foil is good for reheating food, and it can be used to fashion a makeshift skillet over a multi-forked green branch.

88. Shock cords on tent poles last longer if you store them unfolded.

89. A used waterbed mattress filled with air makes a good sleeping pad.

90. An inexpensive sleeping mat can be made from a piece of egg carton foam.

91. Get campfire wood from sawmills, lumber yards or pick up downed timber on public land to avoid paying high prices at campgrounds.

92. Instead of buying brand name or expensive freeze-dried foods, purchase generic bulk items and repack into plastic bags or boxes.

93. Freeze water or soft drinks in plastic milk containers to avoid buying ice on the road.

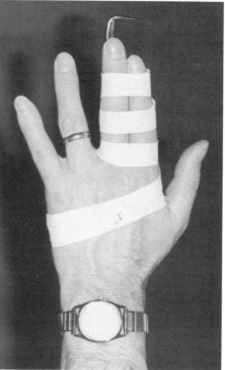

94. Placing a flannel sheet inside a sleeping bag will keep it clean longer, thereby stretching the time between washings.

95. Always set the pace and distance of your daily hikes to the slowest member in your group. This rule is especially important when backpacking with children or elderly people.

96. A pocket comb makes a good splint for a broken finger (left). Simply lay the injured finger and one next to it along the comb and then render immobile with adhesive tape.

97. To make a portable shower bag in camp, fill half a black plastic garbage bag

When tipped over, a canoe doubles nicely as a temporary shelter. With proper support it also makes a good table.

with water and suspend from a tree limb. When the water warms from the sun, punch holes in the bottom to get a steady supply of water.

98. An overturned canoe wedged between two pairs of trees or balanced on logs becomes a temporary table.

99. When buying an ax or hatchet, check the handle tip to see which way the wood grain runs. A vertical grain (in line with the head) is best because it is strong and durable.

100. Suspect ankle sprain on the trail? Afraid to remove the hiking boot until you reach camp? Loosen the laces, then tape a figure 8 pattern from instep to top of foot, around the shin and back. Duct or adhesive tapes works fine, but don't make the wrapping too tight, and get that boot off and the foot in cold water as soon as possible.

III

GETTING THERE

Once you have the gear and understand basic technique, you're ready for a quality camping and backpacking experience. It's a wide world out there—certainly too big to experience in one lifetime—and the opportunities are endless. I have been fortunate enough to travel and camp throughout North America as well as in Europe, Australia, South America and the Caribbean. Camping and backpacking have helped ease the money strain, keeping me out longer, and adding to my experiences in ways that less affordable activities would not permit.

Traveling with a pack on your back or atop a bicycle marks you as a fellow sojourner, admitting you to the universal company of adventure seekers. Occasionally you'll meet the lone wolf who shuns companionship, but for the most part, campers are a gregarious bunch. Driven like moths to candlelight, they flock to the shared campfire, the outpost shelter along the trail, the recreation room at the commercial campground. Camping and RV travel clubs abound, by region in the country, by method of mobility, by special interest, even by type of RV manufacturer. Camping is the most rewarding way to travel and embrace the outdoors.

One of the most enjoyable evenings I ever spent around a campfire occurred on an island on the Quebec side of the St. Lawrence River about twenty years ago. First to arrive in the deserted public campground in late afternoon, I parked my car, set up my small backpacking tent, and broke out fishing gear. When I came back from the river, a couple of walleyes flopping on the stringer in my hand, friendly neighbors to either side of my campsite had arrived.

167

Wilderness or organized campground? Whatever your destination, hiking and camping are hands-on activities.

We exchanged introductions and before long shared our food in a potluck supper. When the stars came out, we sang songs to the accompaniment of a banjo that one of my new friends produced, then played cards under lantern glow until deep into the night.

What was unusual about that experience was this: I was an American driving east to Quebec City, one neighbor was an Englishman heading west on a motorcycle, and the others were a pair of Canadians hitching and backpacking from their home in British Columbia to the Maritimes. Actually, the chance encounter probably wasn't all that strange—similar incidents occur every night in campgrounds and youth hostels throughout the civilized world.

What follows are specific ways to take on the great outdoors and how to make the most of your experience.

CAR, TRUCK OR VAN

A slick way to save money while camping without sacrificing comfort or security is to leave the tent home and turn your car, pickup truck or van into a temporary shelter on wheels.

Organize properly and you can be comfortable, self-contained and mobile. Operating from your vehicle saves time normally spent setting up tents, then breaking down camp and repacking. If you wish, you can drive past designated campgrounds and overnight instead where allowed—some highway rest stops, undeveloped parks and certain other public property, occasionally empty parking lots. You can lock yourself in with all your gear and lock out potential two-legged and four-legged troublemakers.

A mini-van can become a tent on wheels.

Camping in Cars

Unless you own a Suburban with removable seats, a station wagon or other large vehicle where the seats at least fold out of the way, cars and small sport vehicles don't normally provide enough room for comfortable sleeping. They do, however, offer plenty of options for campers on the go. A roof rack, for example, doubles cargo space, and even smaller cars can pull a lightweight utility trailer where you can store your tent and other gear.

At least one manufacturer, Back Country USA, makes a trailer that comes with a tent and 5-by-8-foot covered foam mattress, big enough to sleep two campers. The Back Country Trailer weighs about 500 pounds and is made from heavy-duty, gel-coat fiberglass. The trailer features a 1,000-pound axle, independent wheel movement and 15-inch tires. It costs about $2,500. Less expensive models are available from other companies.

Other suggestions for making creative use of car space:

• Utilize the often-overlooked space under seats when you pack, likewise for the space under a spare tire. It might be large enough for a tool kit.

• Give children a plastic tub for storing souvenirs.

• If you own a sport truck (Chevy S-10 Blazer, Jeep Cherokee, Ford Explorer, etc.) maximize space and ease loading in the bed by laying 1-by-12-inch shelving boards across the wheel wells.

Camping in a Pickup

Friends of mine, retired school teacher Dick Bradley and his wife Shirley, drove 12,000 miles on an Alaska vacation and spent two summer months camping and sleeping in their half-ton pickup truck. Adding a cab-flush topper to their pickup, they loaded it with gear including cookstove, utensils and cookware, foam mattress, sleeping bags and 150 rationed meals and headed out from their Michigan home. The cost for lodging: A couple of nights in motels just for the change of pace.

Inside the topper, the Bradleys added an 18-inch-wide wooden board across the truck bed and against the cab. At night the shelf held their supplies while they stretched out to sleep in the truck bed. As mentioned, placing boards across the wheel wells is another simple way to compartmentalize gear (Chevrolet Fleetside models feature sidewall indentations for double-decking cargo in this manner).

The Soft Shell Truck Tent by Automotive Mailman sets up in the bed of a pickup truck in 10 minutes or less. Four sizes are available.

By adding a cab-level topper to their pickup truck, retired Michigan schoolteacher Dick Bradley and his wife Shirley camped to Alaska and back.

The tailgate on any pickup becomes useful as a cooking platform, table and seat. Adding a padlock to one or both sides of the tailgate renders the topper thief-proof (even with the topper locked, most tailgates can be forced open).

Extended-cab options offer increased comfort and storage space, and slider windows in both the cab rear and topper permit communications with anyone riding in back. Topper considerations include looking at a

The WilderNest Expandable Camper is both a pickup truck topper and a tent.

model with side windows for ventilation and one that can be locked when you must leave the vehicle. To get the best gas mileage, pick a topper that is level with the cab or that is aerodynamically shaped to cut wind.

The fixed-height shell or topper, of course, cramps occupants who are unable to stand. At least two RV companies, Jayco and Sun-Lite, make functional truck toppers (for hauling cargo) that can be cranked up to increase height. And WilderNest Expandable Campers offers a Tent Top model that is neatly self-contained within a fiberglass camper shell. The topper and tent, which can be ordered to fit any model pickup, weigh only 250 pounds in compact size and 325 pounds in full-size truck models. Set-up time is five minutes.

No-frills truck toppers start at about $400 for basic models of aluminum. Used toppers are as low as $100, but finding one not beat up and that will fit your truck and be the right color is another consideration. If you install the topper yourself, buy paper-backed adhesive foam from a supplier, and add a bead of silicone caulk to either side to ensure waterproofing.

Fiberglass toppers are more expensive than aluminum models. The fiberglass shell I bought for my short-bed, extended cab pickup cost $750, but it came with a dome light and controlled-lift door. I spent another $150 for a Yakima roof rack, which allows my wife and me to lash aboard a canoe or tote box containing even more equipment.

Camping in a Van

Keys to making use of available space when truck or van camping include minimizing choices, downsizing when possible, and creative packing. Recently my wife and I rented a Chevrolet Lumina APV van, snapped out the four rear seats, and turned the resulting space into a comfortable shelter during a week-long fishing and camping trip. There was plenty of room for our cooler, portable stove, lantern, duffel bags, tackle and sleeping gear. At night we simply moved equipment to the front seats and rolled out our sleeping bags over a foam pad. Had we been camping with children and wanted privacy, we could have tossed in a small tent for the kids to use.

Commercial conversions for mid-size and full-size vans can be frightfully expensive. But if you're creative and have the time, you can add amenities like window curtains, interior night lights, a compass for the dash, rear windows, a sun roof, interior side shelving, hammocks for little sleepers, bench seats that double as storage lockers for items like a porta potty and portable shower, and exterior racks for water jugs and other bulky items best toted outside.

While visiting campgrounds in France, Germany and England recently, I was impressed with how Europeans are much more creative in their use of space than are North Americans. Caravaning, the Old World term for camping from vehicles, is a popular vacation activity. I saw innovative ideas like canopies zipped to the sides of vans with pop-top roofs that expanded into more sleeping quarters.

The German-built Volkswagen Vanagon is an exceptional vehicle made with camping travelers in mind. An 83-year-old friend of mine has owned seven of these remarkable vehicles, which are equipped with built-in refrigerator and gas range.

Over many years another friend has converted five Ford Econoline vans into specialized vehicles to suit his fishing, hunting and camping needs. With each new van, his first improvement is to glue inch-thick

This Chevrolet Lumina APV van came with its own air compressor.

styrofoam sheets to the interior roof and sidewalls, which he then panels over. This addition quiets the interior and helps retain heat.

A clothes bar is handy for hanging up jackets and overalls, and a four-inch-thick piece of foam rubber is a comfortable mattress. Other touches include wooden shelves and canvas pockets that snap to panels and hold items like maps and gloves, a clothes bar and suspended rod tube rack. A spotlight rigged above the panel doors in back is a tremendous aid at night when my friend wants to load his boat on the trailer.

Heating or cooling your vehicle-turned-bedroom can be accomplished simply by packing an electric fan or heater and attaching to the cigarette lighter by way of a conversion plug. A fully charged spare battery is insurance against running down your vehicle battery. To eliminate the danger of asphyxiation, never burn propane, kerosene or other fossil fuel in your vehicle.

RECREATION VEHICLES

More than 9 million recreation vehicles (RVs) ply the country's roads, and each year another 100,000 Americans join the ranks. Who buys RVs? Today's typical owner is 35 to 54 years old and still works. Many RVs are primary or secondary homes, and that is why they often qualify for federal tax breaks. According to a recent survey, 51 percent of RV owners camped, 31 percent fished, and 20 percent hunted. A total of 16 percent were boaters, and 15 percent enjoyed target shooting.

Many RV owners trace their outdoor experiences to camping from tents. As their families grew, they invested in a small travel trailer, truck or van camper, or folding camping trailer. Bitten by the RV lifestyle, in later years many users trade up to motorhomes, fifth wheels or luxury travel trailers. The industry is currently healthy: At a recent national RV trade

The RVIA estimates that 9 million RVs, including entry-level folding camping trailers, are currently on American roads.

show, nearly 100 manufacturers displayed more than 1,000 RVs. Another 300 suppliers exhibited products.

Citing a University of Michigan study, the Recreation Vehicle Industry Association (RVIA) says of every household that has a vehicle, one in ten is now an RV. Two of every three RV owners plan to buy another model at some point. Average owner expectancy? An amazing seventeen years. Are RVs a good investment? The answer depends on how much you use your RV. Average annual use is forty-four days.

Many owners depend on their RVs year around and not just for camping. Motorhomes and van campers are ideal for moving people, from packing kids aboard for a birthday party at McDonald's to loading seniors for a picnic at the local park. Football fans love RVs for tailgating, and they are especially popular with sportsmen. Full-size van conversions, in particular, make excellent tow vehicles for boats and travel trailers because the rigs are powered by V-8 engines and come with big generators and heavy-duty suspensions and batteries.

Count me among those who love camping and traveling via RV. My first motorhome trip, however, could have been my last. More than twenty years ago during the Arab oil freeze, many Americans were dimming their Christmas lights and doing other patriotic things to cut back on energy consumption. Used RVs swelled resale lots; you could buy an old

RVs like this camper van function as comfortable people movers and are fun to drive.

Coachmen for $200 down. Wheeling a borrowed Winnebago across the country on a long camping trip, I felt a touch sheepish and worried about overusing my credit card to fill the ever-thirsty thing. I should have spared myself the guilt and enjoyed the experience—"the best camping trip ever," according to my kids.

Our family has since towed trailers and driven motorhomes throughout North America. Traveling alone for months on end in motorhomes, I've written two books about my experiences. For me, RV travel is the ultimate perk and a welcome change of diet from a steady menu of tent camping and backpacking. In short, it's the best of both worlds.

RVs are relatively safe and trouble-free if you follow manufacturers' suggestions for driving and preventive maintenance. After many thousands of miles of travel, the problems I have experienced have been minimal: a flat tire in Maine on a small travel trailer, a broken heater hose on another travel trailer in Ontario (which I fixed by snipping excess hose from my car engine), a loose trailer tongue on my dog trailer being towed in Quebec behind our motorhome (not the motorhome's fault).

Seven particular types of RVs fit the broad categories of travel trailers and motorhomes.

Truck Campers

Truck campers are fixed to the bed or chassis of a pickup truck with a load capacity from one-half to one ton. A clear advantage is that when not in use for a period of time, the camper can be separated and stored, freeing up the truck for hauling other things. The disadvantage, of course, is that when you're on the road, you can't leave the camper in the campground and drive off. Another trade-off for their towering height is a dip in gas mileage. On one unit I tested, we lost 20 percent of gas mileage while highway driving.

Manufacturers have become very innovative in recent years, adding plush interiors and modern amenities like refrigerator, stove, kitchen sink and toilet. The Veri-Lite company, for example, recently brought out a 12-foot model with side entry and plush features worthy of a motorhome. A 1993 RVIA survey showed the average sticker price of a truck camper to be $9,195.

Truck campers are less expensive than motorhomes and give families options for travel and destination camping.

The biggest problem most owners have is exceeding the Gross Vehicle Weight Rating (GVWR) by buying a camper too heavy for their vehicle or adding too much weight through passengers and gear. When capacity is exceeded, the engine labors; tires and brakes wear out faster.

Folding Camping Trailers

My love affair with folding camping trailers goes back more than twenty-five years when I honeymooned in a used 1962 Apache, one of the first models ever made. We were kids then and broke and we camped for free at the end of a forest road on Crown land in the wilds of Ontario. Our shelter was warm and dry. The walleye fishing was fantastic, and we had the place to ourselves for a whole week.

Call them fold-downs, pop-ups, pop-tops, soft-tops or what you will, folding camping trailers are an economical way to travel and camp. An RVIA study a few years ago revealed that a family of four would spend $4,000 during a two weeklong airline/hotel vacation or a four week-long car/hotel vacation. The study also found that a family

Several Jayco models of folding camping trailers feature a portable stove which can be set up outside the unit.

vacation involving a car and folding camping trailer was the least expensive of all travel vacations, even cheaper than comparable trips in a truck camper or van conversion.

Properly leveled and loaded, the low-profile trailers (you can usually see over them through your rear-view mirror) are stingy on gas. A few years ago, my family and I spent most of a summer towing a Coleman Valley Forge model for 8,600 miles with our six-cylinder pickup truck. Gas mileage fell only .4 mile per gallon.

Folding camping trailers are mounted on single or dual axles, and they are constructed with collapsible sidewalls of canvas, fiberglass or plastic. Beds on a track system pull out from the compact center on one or both ends to give up to 24 feet of space. Today, a dozen manufacturers make models ranging from bare-bones floor plans to creatively designed plush units with refrigerators, showers, toilets, generous interior and exterior lighting, even air conditioning and 20,000 Btu furnaces.

Most fold-downs are wired to run off either standard, 110-volt electricity or 12-volt car batteries. Refrigerators, hot-water heaters and lights are sometimes fueled by propane, too, and 20-pound bulk tanks last for days and sometimes weeks. Awnings, zip-on add-a-rooms and boat, bicycle and cargo racks are other options. Prices in 1993 ranged from $2,000 to $10,000. The average was $4,352.

Fold downs are a snap to set up and repack for the road—with a little practice, either chore will take only ten minutes or so. Unlike with motor-homes and truck campers, you don't have to haul your sleeping quarters with you every time you get the lookabouts. In cold or wet weather, they are unbeatable for comfort because they're off the ground. And fold-downs require little maintenance. After your trip, run them through the car wash along with your vehicle. Periodically repack the wheel bearings and waterproof the canvas top and sidewalls, if so equipped. That's it and they should last for years.

New models and new options such as stereos, generators and microwaves are coming all the time. Chalet RV Manufacturing offers 15 A-frame style models that include double dinette and sofa-bed layouts. Rockwood, Inc. installs 80-inch-wide mattresses in some of its Cobra units. Columbia Northwest offers a portable whirlpool. Jayco and Vanguard make units with outside-access cargo lockers.

Conventional Travel Trailers

These homes away from home range from 12 feet to 35 feet in length and cost an average of $11,965 new in 1993 although there is also an excellent market for used trailers. All models are towed by means of a bumper or frame hitch. The ideal tongue weight is roughly 10 percent of the GVW. In other words, a 4,000-pound trailer with a tongue weight of 400 pounds is typical, although this figure can vary by as much as five percent either way. If the seller doesn't know GVW you can find out easily by hauling the trailer to a public scales and weighing it twice. First, check the weight of the full unit. Then back it off and weigh just the tongue coupler. That percentage to the GVW is the tongue weight.

Read the owner's manual that came with your vehicle to determine how much weight it can safely tow. Intermediate size and even some compact cars have no problem pulling lightweight trailers under 1,000 pounds, but always follow the manufacturer's recommendations. A reputable trailer hitch company will install the proper hitch for your vehicle and trailer. There are four classes of trailers, each of which may require specialized hitches:

Class 1—2,000 pounds or less
Class 2—2,000 to 2,500 pounds
Class 3—3,500 to 5,000 pounds
Class 4—5,000 to 10,000 pounds

Heavier units typically need a weight-distributing hitch, for example, one that contains equalizing bars. How the unit tracks behind your vehicle will determine if anti-sway bars are needed. Again, the hitch company or trailer dealer can recommend types, along with electric brakes which are controlled from the vehicle. Most larger trailers are equipped with electric brakes.

Heavy-duty safety chains from trailer to tow vehicle frame are standard with most hitches. Cross them, leaving enough slack so they don't hit the ground and don't impede turning. If the hitch fails, the safety chains will allow you to slow the vehicle and eventually stop it.

Fifth-Wheel Trailers

Fifth-Wheel Trailers have a raised forward section that allows a bi-level floor plan. The spacious forward section is most often designed to accommodate

Travel trailers attach to vehicles by way of specialized hitches. Fifth-wheel trailers, which secure to the open bed of a pickup truck, are fast growing in popularity.

the master bedroom. The trailers, which in 1993 cost an average of $18,475 new, are towed by means of a special fifth-wheel hitch in the bed of a pickup truck. These trailers track better than conventional travel trailers because the tongue weight can accept up to 25 percent of the GVW. The reason? The specialized hitch is located right over the pickup's rear axle.

With either type of trailer, as well as large motorhomes, owners may be required to purchase a special state driver's license. In some states the maximum combined length of vehicle and trailer may be only 45 feet. Check with your secretary of state's office for regulations. Many campers prefer to pull their trailers to a designated campground and leave them there all summer. Bigger ones offer all the amenities of home, and manufacturers are constantly coming up with new features. For example, Teton Homes in Mills, Wyoming and Newmar Corporation in Nappannee, Indiana are two companies offering fifth-wheel trailers with double slide-outs, which expand living areas to the size of mobile homes. Carefree of Colorado is a trailer supply company that has a new solar-powered awning panel that trickle-charges a battery while owners sit in the shade or tool on down the road.

Type A Motorhomes

These are constructed on a specially designed chassis. Diesel-powered units are currently growing in popularity and have now captured more than 20 percent of new market sales. Many people live in their Type A motorhomes year-round. Prices range well above $100,000; the average new unit cost $62,583 in 1993.

Options are limitless with the biggest land yachts. Through innovative use of roof space, rear-end racks and special towing packages, many travelers haul everything from backpacks to bicycles, canoes to cars.

Anyone can drive a motorhome or pull a large trailer with a little practice. Safety tips to consider and practice:

• Before committing to parking lots and other confined areas, plan your exit.

• Know that every unit has a blind spot or two, even with the biggest and best of rear-view mirrors. One of the biggest blind spots is usually directly under the windshield.

• Be more aware than normal of what lies ahead, above, behind and to

Know before you go. Some states and many campgrounds enforce length limits on travel trailers and motorhomes.

The aerodynamic shapes and improved engine efficiency of many motorhomes have resulted in better gasoline mileage than in the past. Entry-level units may cost little more than the family car.

the sides. Drivers behind, for example, may not be able to see beyond your vehicle.

• Stay in the right-hand lane when possible, but exercise care along roads without shoulders.

• Allow extra space for turning, and be especially careful when backing up (place a person outside the vehicle for hand-signal instructions when possible). Know that right turns are harder to make than left turns.

• Always keep both hands on the wheel. Gusts of wind and trailer yaw from passing truckers can force you off the road otherwise.

Type B Motorhomes

Also called van campers, Type B motorhomes are essentially panel trucks with a top extension which is either permanent or collapsible. Better-equipped vans feature electricial and water hook-up, sleeping, kitchen and toilet facilities. The average cost of a new unit in 1993 was $39,585. of all RVs they handle best and are the most fun to drive. Gas mileage is often double or more than that of their larger Type A cousins.

For a list of current manufacturers of Type B motorhomes (or any other type of RV), write to RVIA, Dept. CBB, P.O. Box 2999, Reston, VA 22090-0999. The RVIA will send special brochures, including a current copy of *Go Camping America* to readers of this book who include Dept. CBB in the mailing address.

Most RV owners agree that the Type B motorhome, or van camper, is the most fun to drive.

Type C Motorhomes

Sometimes called mini motorhomes or minis, Type C units are usually constructed on a van frame and contain a wide array of conveniences, which naturally dictate price. In 1993, new prices ranged from $29,873 to $38,309.

Better use of space, increased insulation to deaden road noise, improved safety and fuel economy (that Winnebago model I drove in 1974 now gets double the gas mileage), and more efficient appliances are hallmarks of modern small motorhomes. Gone are the boxy rigs of twenty years ago; in their place are sleek, aerodynamically designed units which handle like cars. Propane-burning heaters that shut off automatically if the amount of oxygen drops to an unsafe level are pretty much standard on new models. The furnaces themselves are now up to 99 percent efficient.

The first mini to offer a passenger-side air bag is the Scotty Hilander,

Constructed on a van frame, the Type B, or mini motorhome, is the most popular of motorhome types. As a result, a good resale market exists.

built on the new Dodge Ram chassis by Serro Travel Trailer Co. Exciting new developments occur each year new models debut.

Renting an RV

Before plunking down a huge sum of money for an RV, you might want to rent one to see if the lifestyle is suitable. Look in the *Yellow Pages* under "Recreational Vehicles—Renting & Leasing". For a national directory called *Who's Who in RV Rentals* with more than 400 rental chain outlets, send $6.50 to RVRA, 3930 University Dr., Fairfax, VA 22030 (800-336-0355). Other options are to rent from friends or place an ad in the local newspaper.

Buying a Used RV

To save money, consider buying a used RV. Most dealers warranty their sales after a thorough inspection. Here's what to look for, however, if you buy "as is" (without warranty):

Leakage. This is the biggest problem with used units. Inspect the ceiling and roof for water marks, stains and patch jobs. Run water through the holding tank and faucets and check all connections. If the seller allows, take the RV to a do-it-yourself car wash and hose it down. Window leaks, in particular, will show up.

Appliances. Do the refrigerator, air conditioner, furnace and water pump all work?

Wiring. Inspect all fuses and circuit breakers in the 110 volt system. Is there a 12 volt battery and does it work? How about the outside trailer lights that plug into your vehicle? Any loose wires hanging below the frame?

Seals. Test all latches, locks and seals on doors and windows. Spread soapy water on propane connections to see if they bubble from leaks.

Exterior. Check the tires for lumps, bulges and strange wear patterns that could indicate axle or wheel alignment problems. Is there a spare tire? What are the condition of sewer and water hoses and leveling blocks? Any rust or holes in frame or flooring?

Because fold-downs are so compact and easily stored indoors, be especially wary of used models exposed to the weather for years. If you are buying from a private owner and are not capable of performing a thorough inspection, hire a mechanic to do it for you.

CAMPING BY BOAT

Close your eyes and think of wilderness. The faintest of roads is miles away, and no jet contrails streak the sky. Loons quaver across the island-studded lake from your beach campsite. Your binoculars pick up a wading moose on the far shore; above the animal an eagle pinwheels with the thermals. The eye drifts again from blue sky to green forest. Somewhere beyond that cleft of dark spruce, a river slips

Camping by canoe is an American tradition, more popular today than ever.

from the lake. Tomorrow you will explore that river, the same way you arrived here. By boat.

Boat travel opens up new vistas for campers, but they should wisely prepare their trip before taking to unfamiliar water. Know the lake or river before running it with any kind of watercraft. Get maps, talk to locals, and write to government agencies for as much information as you can gather. Are marinas or other fuel stops along your route? Any designated campgrounds? Then what are the rules for setting up off site? How many portages should you expect along the river, and are the trails clearly marked? Given your skill level, which rapids can be run and which cannot?

Six classes of river navigability, from gentle to near-impassable, are recognized as the International Scale of River Difficulty. Note: If you know which class your target river rates but will be traveling through wilderness, or the water temperature is expected to be below 50 degrees F., the American Whitewater Affiliation recommends advancing the river to the next higher class.

Class I water is easy because the current is gentle, there are few bends, plenty of take-out spots, and a road often runs alongside the flow. Beginners may practice here.

Class II rivers require some skill although the rapids are fairly easy to run because they're less than three feet. Because the river is still fairly wide and predictable, paddlers with intermediate skills can handle it.

Class III rivers are for experienced people. Waves may be five feet high although they are regular and avoidable. Narrow passages require maneuverability skills. Scouting from shore may be necessary.

Class IV water is turbulent with powerful eddies and strong cross currents. Passages are often narrow, and scouting is usually required. Only highly skilled practitioners should attempt such rivers in kayaks, rafts or closed-deck canoes.

Class V water is for experts only who know how to Eskimo roll. Waves are large, irregular and mostly unavoidable. Scouting is a must, and rescue is difficult.

Class VI rivers are extremely dangerous and navigable only by a team of experts who take precautionary measures.

Canoes

Canoes in particular provide the thrill of discovery, the tug of history. "Rivers are the earth's arteries and the oldest highways that ever were," says Verlen Kruger, a neighbor friend of mine who has paddled canoes more than 80,000 miles throughout the Western Hemisphere during the past thirty years. "When early man began to travel the rivers, he made boats that looked much like the canoes of today, 8,000 years later."

As a camper I love how canoes knife me into wild lands and leave no sign, save an occasional prow print along the beach. A canoe can be home to the camper for a single day or for weeks on end. Besides using them for getting into remote areas where foot or motorized accessibility is not practical, canoes are indispensable for floating a lazy suburban stream and pitching a tent for the night.

I have been camping from canoes for thirty years, beginning with the time that forty of us Explorer Scouts loaded twenty canoes into an Algoma Central Railway boxcar. A hundred miles north of Sault Ste. Marie, we waved the train goodbye and spent two weeks fishing, camping and canoeing in the Canadian bush. But I float southern Michigan "civilized" streams, too, including the Grand River near my home. The Grand is one of countless rural/suburban rivers ideal for beginners because of slow currents and the plethora of rental liveries.

Fiberglass, ABS and Kevlar are affordable, durable synthetic materials replacing wood and aluminum in canoes.

Gear checklists and tips on handling a canoe have been covered elsewhere in this book. And, as I have recommended earlier, it is always a good idea to rent expensive equipment before buying it. We are living in a paddlesport renaissance. Because canoes in particular come in many sizes, shapes and materials, it makes no sense to rush out and buy one without first testing a few. After all, you are making an investment that will probably last for many years. Campers especially should think about where they plan to canoe and how much gear they'll want to carry.

First, look at material. I am unaware of any major manufacturers still making canvas canoes, but there are some beautiful, all-wooden models—several from the Old Town company in Maine come to mind—that are no heavier than aluminum, fiberglass or plastics and that are much more durable. However, wooden canoes require periodic upkeep, and at $2,000 or more they are very expensive.

Polyethylene, acrylonitrile butadiene styrene (ABS), DuPont Kevlar and fiberglass are better choices for most of us. These synthetic materials are light to moderate in weight, can take a beating, and require little or no upkeep. Costs range from as low as $400 for a mass-produced polyethylene model to $5,000 for a racing canoe made from Kevlar, the strongest and lightest material available. Some manufacturers use various combinations of synthetics; Mad River, for example, offers a few Royalex (ABS) models featuring handsome ash gunnels and thwarts and seats of cane. Three or four companies even make foldable canoes for packing up and hauling on airplanes.

Aluminum canoes start at about $500 and can cost as much as $1,200. Lightweight and maintenance-free, they are also noisy and stick out in wilderness instead of blending in. A carpet sample or two on the

The author and his wife camp and fish out of a 16-foot aluminum canoe with square end that accepts an electric trolling motor.

floor and a dull coat of paint, however, can help remedy those debits.

If camping or traveling alone, a 14- or 15-foot-long canoe might suffice, but longer canoes are more stable, better streamlined and therefore easier to handle. The 16- and 17-foot models are the most popular for camping. Two people with a lot of gear or who might be hauling heavy game animals should consider a freighter model in 18 or even 20 feet. The square transom on most freighters nicely accommodates a small electric or gas motor, or you can buy side-mounting brackets.

The choice of hull type depends upon intended use, too. If you plan to tackle white water, look for canoes with fore and aft decking and a rocker design with narrow prow for fast turning in rapids. If you'll be paddling or sailing your canoe on big, windy lakes, though, pick a model with pronounced keel and without high-profile prow and stern to catch the wind. Touring and cruising canoes are best suited for the general camper. They usually feature a shallow draft, straight keel line or flat bottom, and are stable and easy to carry. A competent salesman at a canoe specialty shop can explain these and other considerations.

Finding a good used canoe for sale can be tough because even those people who rarely take down their canoes from the garage rafters aren't eager to part with their possessions. If you find a seller, expect to pay at least half the cost of a new canoe. I shopped around for two years before picking up a deal a couple of years ago—a 16-foot aluminum Michicraft for $280. Liveries, by the way, are good places to check because the owners periodically replace their oldest (and usually most beat-up) rentals.

Use your canoe for overnight outings close to home until you gain handling proficiency and learn what to pack and what to leave home. Experience counts here. My wife and I pack "minimum" rather than "maximum" because weight is a key consideration when faced with portages.

Some words about paddles: Buy what is comfortable and does the job for the conditions. Like hiking boots, you may "wear" the paddle for hours and miles—you'll be sore and exhausted much faster from an ill-fit. An old-time guide's method for measuring correct paddle length was to stand erect and hold the paddle lengthwise in front of him. The stern paddle should reach his eyes. The bow paddle should come to that paddler's chin. Today, bow and stern paddles are usually shorter, similar in length, and therefore interchangeable. A shorter paddle with shorter stroke is more efficient—that is, faster and less tiring.

A better method for fitting occurs on the water with the paddler sitting in the canoe. Dip the blade into the water to the throat (where the blade begins to taper into the shaft). The top of the paddle, or grip, should reach your shoulder. The typical paddle length for touring is about 50 inches. For negotiating whitewater on your knees, a longer paddle affords more reach. The best fit, of course, comes through actual use.

Grip style is purely a matter of choice with oval or pear-shaped choices more popular than T-Grip types, which are used for racing and running whitewater. Bent-shaft paddles and those with square blades are also popular with racers because they allow for short, quick strokes. Most camping canoeists prefer paddles with oval-shaped blades, also called beavertails, but square-end paddles can help you cross big water fast. Aluminum paddles with plastic blades are durable and economical but not as light as carbon fiber, which at only 10 or 12 ounces is the choice of racers. Ash, maple and hickory are the toughest woods, but they are also heavy and provide less flex. Many serious canoeists choose laminated paddles, alternating pine or spruce with cedar and reinforced at the ends for greater strength. They also provide excellent flexibility and are light in weight.

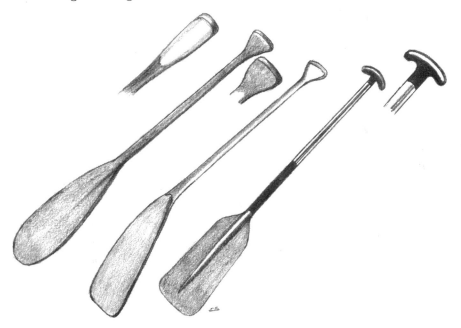

Paddle blade styles include (left to right) oval, bent-shaft and square-end. Grip styles (left to right) are oval, pear-shaped and T-Grip.

On a long trip pack at least one spare paddle and preferably two, mixing the styles. On a 20,000-stroke day you can change off periodically and will always have an extra paddle in case you lose or break one.

Kayaks

At only 13 to 15 feet long, most solo kayaks designed for whitewater are too small for even overnight camping. Open- and closed-decked touring kayaks (now called sea kayaks) from 17 to 21 feet long, however, offer great possibilities for extended camping trips. Certain tandem models may be as long as 23 feet. Models made of fiberglass, Kevlar, polyethylene or ABS are better than collapsible materials for running whitewater. Prices range from $500 to $4,000.

For the Two-Continent Canoe Expedition covering 21,000 miles, Verlen Kruger made his and his wife's 17-foot solo canoes with closed decks and foot-operated rudder systems to closely resemble a kayak. Joining the two craft as a crude catamaran, they paddled and occasionally hoisted sail to cross the Gulf Stream enroute to South America where

Verlen Kruger has paddled more than 80,000 miles, mostly in canoes and modified kayaks he has built himself.

they paddled and camped along the flooded Amazon for seventeen days during one stretch without leaving their canoes. A mosquito netting canopy system that Verlen attached to the canoes protected them.

Narrower than a canoe, though, the typical kayak features a more pronounced rocker and no keel, making it decidedly tippier than a canoe. Even spray shields don't keep out slapping waves, and every river runner knows and expects to use the Eskimo roll—a quick coordinated move of paddle and body to right a flipped-over kayak. For these reasons, plus the fact that the paddler's center of gravity is low—sometimes below the waterline—expect to get wet.

Always wear a helmet, wet or dry suit and lifejacket and store camping gear in floatable, waterproof dry bags front and aft. To improve flotation, some kayaks contain vinyl air sacks, many of which will accept gear and can be sealed watertight. Many feature sealed compartments. A double-bladed paddle is your primary tool; the best ones are made of laminated fiberglass.

Rafts

Inflatable rafts are fun to travel in and camp from. The big rubber doughnuts hold several people at once, yet can be deflated and packed on horses or carried in vehicles. Larger, expedition models with rigid hulls are often placed on a trailer and pulled. Perfect for exploring and running rivers, some types of inflatables accept outboard motors and are ideal for cruising upstream as well as crossing lakes and other big water. They are quite roomy and hold an enormous amount of gear. A 17- or 18-foot model may handle up to a 90-hp engine and take on a payload of 3,000 pounds. One of the world's biggest, a Mark VI Heavy Duty Zodiak, is 23 feet long, will carry 20 people or 6,600 pounds, and may be pushed by a 175-hp outboard.

Better-built rafts contain several layers of tough, nonabrasive fabric impervious to oil and salt and protected from ozone and ultraviolet light. Most inflatables, for example, are made from a heavy-duty nylon or Trevira polyester core material sandwiched between Hypalon and neoprene elastomers, and then finished with Hypalon applied through a high-pressure technique called calendering. Up to six layers of material may be used. Prices from full-line companies range anywhere from $600 for a dinghy to $6,000 or more for an expedition model.

Our most memorable experience while rafting and camping occurred on the South Fork of the Flathead River in northwest Montana when my wife and I joined Damnation Creek Outfitters out of Kalispell for a few days in the Bob Marshall Wilderness. We rode horses in a long packtrain up the river, then rafted and fished for wild cutthroat trout, Dolly Varden and mountain whitefish. Wilderness-use restrictions prohibited anything motorized and required that everything be packed in and packed out. It is amazing how small a package a four-man deflated raft with collapsible floor makes.

The South Fork is a reasonably gentle stream, at least in the twenty-mile section we traveled, but inflatables are capable of handling rougher water if the oarsman is experienced, all gear is stored in dry boxes and lashed tightly, and the passengers hang on. On another trip to the Snake River in Hells Canyon, Idaho, we took on Class IV rapids and got safely wet, but our gear stayed dry. Besides watertight containers, your best friends on a rafting trip are a foot-operated air pump, patch kit and personal flotation device (PFD).

Other Boats

Camping by other types of watercraft such as johnboats and cartoppers, family powerboats and cruisers, sailboats, pontoon craft and houseboats are further fun options. Exploring rivers, chains of lakes, reservoirs, bays and estuaries—even the Great Lakes and oceans—are all possible while camping on shore or islands, or staying aboard the craft itself. Boat camping is one of the best ways to avoid crowded campgrounds and changing your travel plans.

Fuel range and capacity are primary considerations if you'll be in backcountry where there are no marinas or other gas stops. Figure beforehand how much petrol you'll need, then tote at least a 25 percent reserve. Bringing along a spare motor and a good tool kit is also important.

Bigger craft like cruisers and houseboats usually have sleeping quarters and fully equipped kitchens, and you can often tow a smaller boat or toss a dinghy and lash bicycles to the roof. In a sense, the houseboats are like motorhomes or travel trailers. Even though some purists would argue that it is impossible to camp while traveling in a houseboat, tell that to the people who do so and still enjoy setting up a tent or sleeping under the stars.

With any kind of boat, you'll want to pack a spare stove and lantern with fuel, along with a tent for those times when you want to get off the water or away from your traveling companions.

CAMPING BY BIKE

Some motorbike owners have camped for years, packing small side-mount or rear utility trailers for gear and stuffing leftover supplies into saddlebags. The backpacking rage has given bikers new options for mounting backpacks to rear fender racks and adding special sidepacks called panniers. Camping is popular among some motor-cycling clubs whose members are not necessarily rowdy outlaws clad in menacing leather and determined to control campgrounds and ruin your vacation. Many motorcyclists bring their children and enjoy family camping, too.

The pedal-powered sports are in these days, and what better way to get in physical shape than cycling cross-country or scrambling up a mountainside? Why not tote along a lightweight backpacking tent and basic camping gear, too? The old English 10-speed bicycle hanging from your garage rafters is fine for overnight camping, but serious bikers spend big bucks on specialty bikes designed to handle about anything that the highways or Mother Nature serves up.

Road bikes run the price gamut from put-it-together-yourself models for $150 to $1,000 super-light aluminum dandies with Shimano 700 CX components. Long-distance tour riders who camp look for light-weight, road-eating suspensions, pedal toe clips, drop handlebars, all-weather tires with minimum resistance, comfortable saddles and responsive handling. Again, test or borrow before you buy.

More than 40 million people are estimated to ride mountain bikes although most of them don't venture into rough terrain. When you do decide to jump logs, take on hairpin turns, scramble in scree and skirt rocks, you'll want a strong bike made from aluminum, carbon-fiber or chrome-moly alloy. Other needs: beefy suspension, handlebars that flare out and up, multi-gear drive train, quick-shift levers and fat, knobby tires. Entry-level mountain bikes cost as little as $250, but you can pay nearly 10 times that amount, too.

Bikers who camp need to haul gear, of course. A lightweight day or fanny pack may be fine for incidentals, but you don't want 40 pounds on your back while trying to maintain your balance on skinny tires or negotiating a steep-sloping trail. Fender-mount bags are the way to go. A good example is the Chaos Crag Pannier from Overland Equipment. Designed for rear bike racks, the pannier affords 2,630 cubic inches of storage space for a small tent, food and other gear. Equipped with a foam bottom and internal support, the tapered Cordura bag stands alone and can be toted by its web top handle or slung over the shoulder with a special strap. Zippered pockets and a rear mesh pocket provide creative

Today's mountain bikes and road bikes handle most terrain and deliver lightweight campers wherever they want to go.

storage options, and the bag top comes with sculpted hood to keep out dirt and water.

Other specialty bags attach to the seat, and a set of handlebar forks provide a rack for a fishing pole and hiking staff. A tire repair kit, frame-mounted water bottle, good road maps and raingear are essentials to pack. Review the backpacker's checklist for other considerations.

CAMPING BY PACK ANIMAL

Coming into camp at dusk on the downbound trail, I watched the horse in front of me throw occasional sparks when his iron-shod hooves clipped a rock. My own mount, a roan mare named Rosie, hugged the mountain wall, away from the edge and a quarter-mile of free fall to the rushing South Fork of Montana's Flathead River. Rosie sighed in a loud neigh. She had traveled this narrow trail many times before, and now she was tired and wanted her grain and me off her back. I wanted off, too. It had been a long day of rafting and fishing here in the million-square-acre Bob Marshall Wilderness. My arms were tired from catching cutthroat trout. My legs were sore from riding Rosie. Night's chill was coming on.

Never did a campfire feel cozier and a sirloin steak taste better than what we dozen campers experienced that evening. I don't own a horse— don't want the expense of buying and maintaining a horse—but once a year it's fun to head for Nevada, Colorado or Montana and hire an outfitter to provide the animals and supply the wranglers and a great cook to do all the work. Although such a wilderness experience is expensive compared to other kinds of camping, it's an American safari vacation you never want to end.

Other advantages to riding and packing with horses, mules, burros and even llamas: You can go in deeper, pack more gear, and you don't have to carry any of it yourself.

Opportunities abound and not just in Western states and provinces. There may be horse-riding trails with designated campgrounds close to home. In my home state of Michigan, for example, the Shore to Shore Riding-Hiking Trail from Lake Michigan to Lake Huron is popular. Horse owners often travel in groups, trailering their steeds to either end of the marked route, then spend from three days to a week riding among sand dunes and forests across the state. Most riders don't string pack animals; instead, someone is assigned to drive ahead and set up camp.

If you're new to riding, you'll want to practice at a commercial stable at home. A lesson or two will help (see Part II for tips on handling a horse) and may ease saddle soreness. Other than hard-heeled footwear, you don't need any special clothing (forget the spurs, chaps and 10-gallon cowboy hat—standard garb of Western movies) although a billed cap and three-quarter-length rain parka with a hood are comfortable options in rain.

State and provincial tourism departments as well as regional and local chambers of commerce have information on outfitters.

WINTER CAMPING

The demand for physical exercise so in vogue today extends to winter outdoor activities, including camping. People who like to ice fish, hunt, cross-country ski and snowshoe are finding that winter camping is a great way to avoid the crowds and biting insects of summer. Some parks and recreation areas are open all winter. Commercial campgrounds operating twelve months of the year often slash winter rates by half those of summer.

Inuit hunters and trappers who travel by snowmobile and dog-sled

Many hard-core backpackers have taken to cross-country skiing as a means of extending their camping activities through the winter.

team are used to overnighting in sub-zero temperatures. These same methods of transportation are open to the winter recreationist who camps. Most, however, will either overnight in their motorhomes or set up a tent camp while operating from their car. But the most inexpensive, quiet and solitary fun is experienced by those who snowshoe or cross-country ski.

Snowshoes

Snowshoes, which likely originated in Asia with native hunters in forested areas, have been around for at least two millennia. They offer a traditional, romantic way to get around in winter landscape. Although

**Snowshoes are ideal
for getting around in
winter when snow
accumulates to 12
inches or more.**

progress is slow when compared to snowmobile or dog team—even Nordic-ski travel is faster—what's the point of hurrying if your goal is to embrace solitude and beauty? For the foot camper, snowshoes are ideal because he can tote a heavy pack, and his slower progress and wider means of support translate to better balance and fewer spills than the cross-country skier is likely to experience.trail-off into margin.

Useful when at least a foot of snow blankets the ground, snowshoes become more valuable as snow depth increases. Break in slowly to this leg-powered activity, and make sure the shoes are appropriate in size to your weight with pack. On a winter excursion in the White Mountains of New Hampshire, I borrowed a pair of snowshoes that didn't fit me right, forcing me to throw wide my hips. When we reached our destination that evening, a Forest Service cabin, the temperature inside was 3 degrees. Although we warmed up the place, I slept poorly. Next morning my back was out and I could barely walk even without snowshoes.

The *Alaskan* model is the fastest, longest and narrowest of three key types. Typically about 10 inches wide, models may be 5 feet or longer, have turned-up toes and long tails. Ideal for mushing heavy loads in open country, the Alaskan also goes by various other names, including pickerel, cross-country, Yukon and Arctic.

The *Michigan* or Maine snowshoe (sometimes called Algonquin) is wider at 12 to 14 inches and somewhat shorter at 3 to 4 feet. This shoe, which has a slightly upturned toe and also features a tail, is better suited for negotiating brushy terrain.

Bear paw snowshoes are basically oval in shape with the toe end being somewhat wider than the heel end. A typical pair will measure 13 inches by 33 inches each. Various modifications are called—what else but—modified bear paw and Green Mountain snowshoes. Bear paws are the easiest to use, even though they feel like you're wearing giant pancakes the first time out.

Although aluminum and various man-made materials are coming on the market all the time, the best snowshoes continue to be made from fine-grain white ash. Webbing and lacing are evenly split between rawhide and nylon-reinforced neoprene.

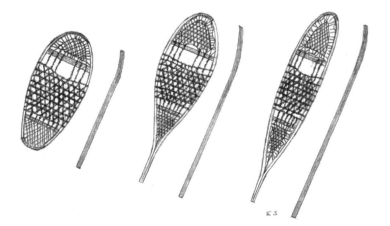

Snowshoe types include (left to right) bear paw, Michigan and Alaskan.

Cross-Country Skis

Snow skiing, which has its origins in Scandinavia, has been around for at least 4,000 years. Some 800 years ago Norwegian soldiers relied on skis for military reconnaisance. Today, they are a great way to stretch your winter fun into overnight camping far from the plowed road.

New material developments have produced a plethora of choices besides wood, and you can buy waxless skis which have a permanent

Cross-country skis and poles differ slightly in length and width according to their intended purpose. The illustration shows proper sizing for classical skis.

pattern of diamond, step, fishscale or mohair to give them traction in various kinds of snow. Some people still prefer to wax their skis to exacting conditions for maximum glide. What started out as touring or basic Nordic skis has evolved into three main kinds.

Classical skis of medium width are used in and out of groomed trails. They are ideal for beginners and best suited for winter campers who want to stick with the basic kick-and-glide method of locomotion. Proper length occurs when the skis, stood on end, reach the wrist of the person whose arm is stretched vertically. Poles are typically shoulder height.

Regardless of type, camber is the amount of bow in the ski when it lies flat on the floor. Terrain and weight (wear your loaded pack when selecting) dictate the right size of ski and correct stiffness of camber. To determine it, a person should be able to pull out a sheet of paper with minimum resistance from under the foot of another person standing in the skis. Transfer all the weight to one ski and the paper should hold fast.

Because *freestyle* skis are faster and designed for groomed trails, they are used for racing. A little shorter than classical skis, they are mated with longer poles that are nose-high. Many people move up to freestyle skis once they become familiar with the sport. Low-cut shoes with flexible bindings are standard these days.

Cross-country downhill skis and equipment resemble that of their alpine cousin: metal-edged wider skis slightly shorter than classical models, rib-high poles, more sturdy boots and bindings. They're ideal for getting into backcountry with steep terrain, but campers should be fairly proficient skiers before investing in a pair.

Follow these suggestions to turn your winter camping trip into a fun adventure on snowshoes or Nordic skis:

- Never travel or camp alone
- Travel single file.
- Take turns breaking trail.
- Travel a reasonable distance. Don't overestimate your ability
- Dress in layers and carry a small backpack for holding clothing you don't need at the moment.

BACKPACKING

Even now, thousands of years after an early linguist carved symbols in clay with a sharp stick, we are still beasts of burden. No one understands that better than those of us who spend an inordinate amount of time outdoors. We have to pack clothing, raingear, food, cookware and utensils, items for our safety, more gear attendant to sport: fishing tackle; binoculars, camera and accessories for bird watching; bow, quiver of arrows or firearms and ammo for hunting.

Of course, we can always load the equipment into cars, trucks, canoes, toboggans, snowmobiles or saddlebags and ride instead of walk. But that would spoil the whole idea of easing into wilderness with the minimum amount of stuff we need to survive and yet be comfortable on our backs. Backpacking is a special challenge that makes us think through our abilities and—taken to its ultimate expression back of beyond—live by our wits. We step softly and compete with ourselves, not with Nature. The farther the car fades into the distance, the more we test self-reliance and personal limits. We get a physical and an emotional high. We learn. We come back and do it again.

My first experience with backpacking—not the knapsack and canteen adventures of my youth but honest-to-goodness backpacking with a real pack, flyweight tent, freeze-dried food and stuffed (not rolled up) sleeping bag—occurred in Colorado in 1978 when a friend and I took my two youngsters into the Rockies. We camped in a cirque where beargrass and lupine grew and whose lush meadow was seamed by a flashing mountain stream flanked with watercress.

That evening as we cooked supper on our two-pound stove, we watched three bears—a cinnamon and two blacks—forage along the mountainside across from our camp. Under the vault of nighttime sky, the kids found and identified some of the constellations they had studied in science class but didn't get to see while living in the city. We slept

Interest in the environment and the need for physical exercise are reasons why backpacking has grown so popular. New recruits also cite the high they get from becoming self-reliant.

happy and warm even though by morning frost had covered the rainfly, and ice had tightened a wide bend in the stream outside our door. We caught cutthroat trout for breakfast, watched pikas watch us from their home in the talus slide, and identified mountain birds and flowers.

We never saw another person for three days. I was hooked on backpacking.

According to the Red Wing Shoe Company, the typical person walks 65,000 miles—a distance approaching the earth's circumference three times—in his or her lifetime. Walking is wonderful exercise for lifelong health. It reduces stress, restoring rhythm and balance to a hectic day full of tension. As a writer, I find that walking affords critical transition, helping me to empty out my mind from a story recently completed and filling the space with ideas and words for the next. Walking can be done anywhere. It is free.

Where to go backpacking? Not only are many of the nation's campgrounds growing crowded, but an increasing number of people are taking to public trails, too. The stampede has forced rangers to close popular areas of some parks and forests and limit camping to designated sites on other properties. The secret here is not to be a crowd follower, but that does not mean you must escape to wilderness in order to have a quality experience. Excellent backpacking opportunities await suburban hikers along abandoned railways, river corridors, even urban parks that connect with one another.

On many long-distance hikes such as along the Appalachian Trail and the Lewis & Clark Trail, you can retrace history. All states have trail information for hikers and backpackers—contact the parks or recreation division of your state's department of natural resources, conservation department or game and fish department. Hiking clubs abound, too. For additional details, consult the Appendix.

CAMPING IN PUBLIC CAMPGROUNDS

If you spent your lifetime camping at a different designated campground each night, you probably wouldn't have to repeat any of your stays. If that possibility did occur, you could simply get a permit from the park ranger and head for the backcountry. Public campgrounds are managed by federal, state and local agencies, most of which are connected with parks, forests or recreation divisions of government. For more information, see the Appendix.

National Parks

Some 225 locations found in 71 million acres managed by the 10 regional offices of the National Park Service include national parks, lakeshores and seashores and recreation areas. The first, Yellowstone National Park (1872) remains one of the most popular, along with Yosemite and Glacier national parks. Cape Cod National Seashore in Massachusetts and Grand Portage National Monument in Minnesota are other examples of parks where camping is permitted. Entrance fees are charged in addition to camping fees.

National Forests

The U.S. Forest Service manages more than 4,000 mostly rustic campgrounds scattered throughout 191 million acres in 41 states. Possibilities range from grassland camping in the Plains states to rugged mountain peaks and deserts in the West to deep woods in the North and East to tropical settings in the South. No entrance fees are charged, and roughly 60 percent or more than 2,700 campgrounds are free. Most have hand-pumped drinking water, portable vault toilets, fire rings, picnic tables and trash collectors. Designed to blend into the environment, the campgrounds are located on or near water. Know that motorhomes and other

Many of the more than 4,000 national forest campgrounds are located on or near water.

RVs longer than 22 feet will have trouble negotiating roads in these forest campgrounds.

U.S. Army Corps of Engineers

The Corps is in charge of more than 93,000 campsites on or near water. Many of these, along with other boat launching ramps and outdoor facilities, are explained in ten brochures called "Lakeside Recreation."

Bureau of Reclamation

This agency oversees 300 recreation areas in seventeen Western states through five regional offices. Brochures and maps are available.

Bureau of Land Management

The BLM has control of 270 million acres, or about 40 percent of federal public land. Most BLM land is found west of the Mississippi River. More than 2,000 sites have been built or planned for outdoor recreation, including camping.

Tennessee Valley Authority

At least one of the 400 TVA recreation sites in seven southern states is located within a day's drive of half the American population. The states include Tennessee, Kentucky, North Carolina, South Carolina, Georgia, Alabama and Mississippi. A free master brochure entitled "Recreation on TVA Lakes" along with fifteen reservoir maps is available.

National Wildlife Refuges

Many of the more than 360 national wildlife refuges, which are managed by the U.S. Fish & Wildlife Service, allow camping. Altogether the refuges total more than 90 million acres. Individual brochures are available at no cost for most of these properties.

Camping fisher-
men relax at a state
forest campground
in Michigan. Basic
amenities include
a picnic table, fire
ring, hand water
pump and toilets.

State and Local Public Lands

For camping opportunities and other outdoor information in your state or
province, contact the department of natural resources, conservation
department or game and fish department responsible for management.
More than half of the fifty state forestry divisions have some sort of outdoor
recreation program, which includes camping and backpacking. State and
provincial agencies manage parks within their respective jurisdictions.

CAMPING CLOSE TO HOME

Campers don't always have to travel far to enjoy a great outdoor experience. The dictionary defines "remote" as far away, secluded, dis-
tant and far removed, yet you can enjoy "remote" camping practically in

your own backyard if you look around. I've enjoyed the same feelings of peacefulness I get on a mountaintop while getting away from it all in a county park 10 miles from home. Remoteness is often more a state of mind than place anyway. It means leaving behind a world of people pressure and video-game violence and escaping to a spot where you can be relatively alone. Such places do exist and not just in wilderness.

Municipal and County Campgrounds

A good spot to start looking is in the local *Yellow Pages* under "Campgrounds." Municipal, township and county campgrounds not far from home are often small, both in size and cost. Usually overlooked by those on the road, they offer seclusion and a quiet weekend away from home— even if home is only across town.

I keep an eye out for these "pocket campgrounds" whenever I'm traveling, too. Passing through a town at day's end, I'll often ask a store clerk, police officer or gas-station attendant if there is a municipal park nearby where camping is allowed. Accommodating perhaps only ten to twenty-five families, these government-run campgrounds may be older and without electrical and water hookups for RVs. Consequently, they rarely fill up. The lack of certain modern conveniences and local government subsidies keep camping fees to a minimum.

A township park along Michigan's famed Au Sable River was a popular spot for my family for years. We had the place to ourselves for only a few dollars per night. Another time we were returning from a six-week camping trip to the West. We spent Friday night at a big commercial campground in South Dakota, miles from anywhere but still filled to capacity with a noisy weekend crowd. Exhausted from a long day on the road, we retired early. Sometime after midnight the party crowd settled down.

Next day we found a small municipal campground in Crookston, Minnesota. Only two or three other campsites of the twelve or fifteen available were occupied even though it was a Saturday night. With the money saved, we enjoyed a movie at a theater within walking distance. Settling in for a quiet night's sleep, it seemed strange that we had to return to civilization in order to find a remote, peaceful spot to camp.

The manager of a local campground not far from where I live tells me that 85 percent of his business is from locals. "We used to be an overnight stop for people on the go," he explained. "Now we get few over-the-road campers, and most of our business is repeaters."

Commuter Camping

Commuter camping? Doesn't "commute" mean travel between home and work? Yes. But when commuters camp, the campground becomes their temporary home away from home. It's perfect for families when both parents work and can't arrange schedules or when the key bread earner is working overtime and can't afford to take a week off. Given the trend of shorter family travel vacations, commuter camping works for stay-near-home vacationers. Some commuters spend the whole summer at such campgrounds, moving their site every ten to twelve days to satisfy local regulations. Reversing the normal order of vacations, they return home on weekends to check the house and look after things.

Here's a typical scenario: Dad gets up at six o'clock and showers and shaves in the bath house, which is empty except for a couple of other working campers. Some mornings he'll make coffee and breakfast. This morning it's raining and even though he could prepare a meal in the nearby pavilion, he'll eat on the road and let the family sleep. He arrives at work at 7:30, his mind clear, his body rested.

The rain stops by 9:00 A.M. Mom, who has the week off, and the two kids—ages eight and eleven—wake to sunlight. Over breakfast, they discuss the day's possibilities: raspberry picking at a nearby farm, a trip to the county library, shopping at the town mall, a free tour of a local dairy farm. Later, while the kids are swimming under the watchful eye of the campground lifeguard, Mom prepares a casserole for the potluck supper. Tonight is Tuesday, community campers night, when families make new friends.

Dad returns from work by four o'clock and takes a nap. At 5:30 supper is served. He discovers another camper who is as crazy about bass fishing as he. After supper the two dads and their sons try the quiet lake for largemouths. Later, as woodsmoke drifts through the campground and lanterns throw soft yellow light, the family toasts marshmallows outside their tent. After a mock show of protest, Mom agrees to strum a few tunes on her guitar.

The crackling fire creates shadows on nearby birches, and skybound sparks look like platoons of fireflies. One youngster counts satellites crossing the heavens; the other tallies shooting stars. "You'd never guess we're only seven miles from home," Dad says as the family turns in and the lantern sputters to silence.

GUIDED CAMPING ADVENTURES

Many people seek high adventure in unusual or exotic places where camping may be by design or necessity. Either way, camping is the best chance you'll have of seeing a land from the inside out. A cultural tour of Uruguay, an archaeological dig in the Middle East, a natural history sail among the Galapagos Islands, an Alaska river adventure by raft or kayak.

A friend of mine wanted to do something that wasn't her run-of-the-mill vacation. Interesting possibilities included a float trip down the Rhine River in Germany and hot-air ballooning over France's wine country. Then she learned she could go to Kenya on a photo safari for two weeks for the same price. So she joined fifty-three others on a jungle camping expedition sponsored by the Smithsonian Institution. "I learned a lot about the people and about Africa, but I actually learned more about me," she said. "After the trip I decided to return to school and study a foreign language."

Many of these trips allow, indeed demand, outdoor physical activity, which is a big reason they are growing in popularity. How do you choose the right adventure camping trip? How much should you pay? Months after you have leafed through the outfitter or booking agent's dazzling full-color brochure and you are trekking across the Arctic with a band of Inuit seal hunters is not the time to wonder if the people who arranged your adventure are reputable. Always ask for references, and then talk to people who have gone. Here are some examples of companies and the adventures they offer:

This Sobek rafting and camping adventure occurred on the Bio-Bio River in Chile. The raft is about to enter Lost Yak Rapids.

The National Outdoor Leadership School (NOLS) prepares two-week to fourteen-week courses in outdoor skills for students aged sixteen and up. More than 30,000 young people have graduated. The courses tend to be rigorous, but they vary in physical difficulty. Their purpose is to give members an appreciation of the environment while teaching them to become safe, skilled backcountry travelers. Sometimes the courses include sea kayaking in California and Alaska or mountain climbing in Alaska, Africa or South America. In the U.S. NOLS courses are run in eighteen national forests, twenty-one national parks and preserves, and on BLM land in seven states.

The National Audubon Society Expedition offers hands-on wilderness experiences where students gain an appreciation of the social and natural environment. Groups of eight to twelve students (from eighth-graders through adults in graduate school), along with two instructors, enjoy hiking, camping, canoeing, backpacking, outdoor cooking and exploring in Maine, the Pacific Northwest, New England, the Southwest, Newfoundland and Labrador.

The government of the Northwest Territories offers tremendous opportunities for active adventure trips. Consider a ten-day dog-sled trip to

Igloolik on the Melville Peninsula, backpacking from several days to several weeks in Auyuittuq National Park, a six-day trek to the North Pole, camping for eleven days on Ellesmere Island, two weeks of whitewater rafting on the McKerand River, or a ten-day wildlife tour on Baffin Island.

Sobek's International Explorers Society offers a full range of easy to strenuous expeditions to remote regions of the world. The trips are geared toward an instructive, active approach to travel, and they emphasize encounters with the people, histories and environments of places visited. The company applies a five-point rating scale to its trips from Class I (Easy) to Class V (Strenuous). Camping and hiking are integral activities of Class III (Average) and higher experiences. Class V expeditions often explore uncharted rivers or tackle mountain peaks of 18,000 feet or higher.

Besides writing to these and other companies (see the Appendix), check the classified ads in *Outside, Backpacker* and other specialty magazines.

ON YOUR OWN IN FOREIGN LANDS

The world is a shrinking place, and most of it is accessible from major cities within twenty-four hours. Camping and backpacking are the best ways to stretch your travel dollar and to experience life the way the people who live there do. Opportunities for travel to Eastern Europe, Russia and China are especially exciting because they are so new.

With the exception of Canada and Mexico, wherever you travel you'll need a valid U.S. passport. A passport will take six to eight weeks to be issued after filing an application. Applications are available from any state or federal court authorized to naturalize aliens and from U.S. State Department offices in large American cities. Main post offices may have them, too.

For information on customs regulations, write to the U.S. Government Printing Office, Washington, DC 20402, and ask for the pamphlets "Customs Hints for Returning U.S. Residents" and "Know Before You Go." You might want to consider camping insurance, too, available from most automobile clubs.

Camping in Europe

If traveling to Europe, another suggestion is to secure an International Camping Carnet. Most European campgrounds are privately owned, and the carnet, which is actually another document of identification, is recognized by campground owners. Some require that you leave either the carnet or your passport with them until all bills are paid. The carnet also provides for third-party public liability insurance while you camp, and it usually entitles you to preferential treatment (including price discounts). To get one for a fee, before leaving home, contact the National Campers and Hikers Association, 7172 Transit Rd., Buffalo, NY 14221 (716-634-5433). The cost covers husband, wife and all children under eighteen. Send birthdates, birthplaces and correct names and addresses for all family members.

Competition among domestic and foreign airlines makes for attractive prices and periodic price wars especially at times other than the busy summer season. Most transcontinental flights allow for up to forty-four pounds of baggage per person. That amounts to a lot of camping equipment if you carefully choose for space and weight.

You can often buy or rent camping gear in foreign lands. Stores I have visited in Paris, London and Edinburgh, for example, were well stocked with everything a backpacker or car camper would need. You can even rent an RV (called "caravans" in Europe), but be advised that although most European campgrounds feature water and electricity hookups, many lack sewer hookups. Because Europeans love to camp, though, campgrounds abound throughout the continent. Most have adequate shower and toilet facilities, with small grocery stores on the grounds. In Scandinavian countries, you might even get a sauna.

Non-motoring campers can save money by staying at youth hostels, which are plentiful throughout Europe (France alone has more than 300). To plan thoroughly your camping trip, write to each country's national tourist office. You can obtain the New York City office addresses and telephone numbers of most by calling directory assistance at 212-555-1212 or 800-555-1212. You can also contact the national camping club offices (addresses in the Appendix) of the countries you plan to visit.

Caravaning is popular among European camping families. The author photographed this scene in England.

Youthful backpackers have known for a generation that the most inexpensive way to see Ireland (where the author took this photo) and the rest of Europe is to carry everything on your back.

Camping in Canada

Canada was designed for campers. Some 90 percent of her shore-to-shore expanse is still wilderness, yet her cities are modern, throbbing magnets of discovery. Contained within are a million lakes, excellent roads, more than 2,000 campgrounds, 28 national and some 300 provincial parks. The ones I have visited over the years are clean, untrampled and inexpensive, especially given the U.S. dollar's favorable currency exchange rate of recent years.

Quebec City and Montreal offer the best of old and new worlds. Nova Scotia has her desolate strands of seashore and hungry tides that lick their way up rugged inlets. Toronto may well be North America's most cosmopolitan city. Manitoba and Saskatchewan feature boundless skies, fields of wheat and rapeseed, and a history of settlement only 100 years old. Alberta, where the cowboy ethic runs strong, is the California of western Canada. British Columbia boasts a half-dozen mountain ranges, 1,000 miles of seascape, and Michigan-sized Vancouver Island. The Yukon and Northwest territories draw sportsmen today the way they lured goldseekers a century ago.

The author found this huge glacier in Alberta's Banff National Park well worth the climb to see and photograph.

Be sure to carry a birth certificate or voter registration card for each person in your party as well as registration certificates for all vehicles, including trailers. If traveling with a rental unit, carry a letter of authorization from the owner. Your insurance company will issue a Canadian Non-Resident Interprovince Motor Vehicle Liability Insurance Card. Besides the wonderful support literature that government tourism offices provide, you can find hundreds of private campgrounds by looking through *Woodall's North American Campground Directory.*

Camping in Mexico

For travel south of the border, get a free tourist card, available from any Mexican Consulate as well as most travel agents and airlines servicing Mexico. The tourist card functions as your passport, and although it is not actually required in border towns, you would be wise to secure one and keep it with you at all times. The port of entry will issue a Vehicle Permit. Back that up with your vehicle registration and title, including a notarized statement from the owner authorizing your use of a vehicle other than your own. You will also have to buy Mexican auto insurance, available from competing companies along the border.

Although camping is not popular with Mexicans, there are lots of campgrounds. However, they are often lacking in facilities, and the water may not be safe to drink. If traveling with an RV, fill your water tank before crossing the border, or drink only bottled water. Supermarkets in large cities can supply food needs, and hardware and paint stores stock some camping gear, including propane and liquid camping fuel.

You will find trailer parks featuring showers, laundry facilities and convenience stores along highways and outside major cities. Tenters, usually welcome, are advised to stay in these organized sites rather than strike out on their own. Lone campers are asking for trouble from banditos. One popular and quite safe area is along the Pacific Coast at Mazatlan.

National parks in some of Mexico's most scenic spots are on the increase. These are found throughout the country in areas of rugged mountains, forests, streams and lakes. Facilities, however, are usually lacking. A good information source is *Rand McNally's Campgrounds and Trailer Parks in Mexico.* The American Automobile Association (AAA) also has a directory of major campsites for members. I know of no youth hostels in Mexico, but backpacking is growing in popularity among those who wish to see the country on foot (don't travel alone, however). Much of Mexico remains to be discovered, and camping is an ideal way to do it.

Camping in the Caribbean

Some thirty sun-soaked islands from Aruba to the U.S. Virgin Islands beckon campers to the Caribbean. Hopscotch to them or any of the 700 islands in the Bahamas group and you will hear French, English, Dutch and Spanish spoken as well as dialects—French Creole, Dutch Papiar,

Irish brogue, Scottish burr. Because entry requirements differ from island to island, it is best to check with the government customs and tourism departments of each. Most maintain New York tourist offices. Be sure to inquire about camping, which has become increasingly popular. The Jamaica Tourist Board, for instance, issued a press release some years ago announcing that campers can enjoy a one-week vacation there for as little as $100 each ($150 to $200 today perhaps), including food, accommodations and island transportation. Popular camping resorts on Jamaica alone have more than 1,000 campsites for rent.

On St. John, smallest of the three U.S. Virgin Islands, the National Park Service oversees Cinnamon Bay Campground which is operated by a concessioner who provides 10-by-14-foot tents, camp cots with pads, and other gear. Hiking, Jeep tours, swimming, snorkeling and fishing are activities my wife and I enjoyed on a recent visit. Many other opportunities await Caribbean campers. Dominica, for example, offers jungle camping, and St. Lucia features mountain climbing and camping on the twin-peaked Pitons.

Citizens of the U.S. can travel quite freely with no more documentation than a birth certificate or voter registration card. A passport is the best insurance, however, and travelers might also want to consider a visa or tourist card.

Camping in Australia

All visitors to Australia need a passport and entry visa, which are available through the government's embassies and consular offices. Nearly the size of the U.S., the world's smallest continent and largest island contains only 17 million people, mostly living in a handful of southeast seacoast cities. Australia's wide-open interior, the Outback, is rife with backpacking and camping opportunities although the arid land can be inhospitable and settlements are far apart. Even train travel may take three days from east to west.

Backpacking is very popular among young foreigners. Americans in particular are generally welcome. On a recent trip to Sydney and the Blue Mountains, my college-age daughter and I found plenty of low-cost backpacking hotels and youth hostels. Destination campgrounds and other amenities, however, are hard to come by except in national and provincial parks. But a large number of organized camping adventures arranged by outfitters include whale watching, snorkeling and diving on the Great Barrier Reef, Outback trekking, and kayaking crocodile-infested mangrove swamps.

Camping in Other Parts of the World

Unless you're an experienced traveler, you would be wise to contract with an outfitter to camp and backpack in most other foreign lands. Language differences, unfamiliar national laws, and strange local customs may initially attract the adventuresome, but they also easily frustrate and can endanger the inexperienced. Foreign travel begins with a mindset to go with the flow and not impose your attitudes or values on others. It ends with an experience—good or bad— but always memorable.

Whether your journey takes you to the South American Andes, the African plains, the jungles of Malaysia, or the shores of Russia's Lake Baikal, prepare for the adventure as though you're studying for final exams. Preparing for a fishing/camping trip to the steamy jungle of southern Venezuela, I had my doctor call the Center for Disease Control in Atlanta, Georgia, to inquire about disease-prevention measures. As a result, he gave me a shot for yellow fever and prescribed anti-malarial tablets called Larium. I didn't see a mosquito during my adventure, but having taken the necessary precautions gave me reassurance.

That word, reassurance, is always relative because a person never knows who he'll meet along the trail, what experiences await him at the next campground.

CAMPING ON A BUDGET

One of the reasons I've always camped is because, short of mooching off relatives or jumping slow-moving trains, it's the best way I know to vacation on a budget. Go figure: A family of four on a week's sojourn will spend at least a grand if they shell out a daily average of only $50 on motels ($350), $50 in restaurants ($350), and $40 or so ($300) for incidentals such as souvenirs and theme-park admissions.

This figure can be considerably higher. A friend of mine recently blew $6,000 (including airfare) on a two-week family vacation to the Cayman Islands. "Can you recommend a good four-person tent?" he asked. "Next year we're going camping and save some money."

Even if you travel to exotic places like the Caribbean, you can squeeze the bucks by camping. The lowest-priced cottage my wife and I could find to rent for a week on St. John in the Virgin Islands—a cottage miles from the beach, by the way—cost more than $900. By comparison, a roomy tent, fully equipped with cots, bedding, lantern, stove, cooler and cooking utensils (on the beach at Cinnamon Bay Campground) cost about one-third or $350.

Beating Eating Costs

There is no reason that food prepared and eaten in camp has to cost more than at home. In fact, it can be cheaper if you have any prowess as a hunter or fisherman and know how to identify safe, natural foods like spring greens, summer berries and fall mushrooms. Doing so may be healthier than eating packaged or prepared foods because some greens lose up to one-third of their vitamins within an hour of picking.

Planning meals ahead of time encourages campers to shop for sales items weeks in advance and skirts what might otherwise be a budget strain. Spaghetti, chili and meat loaf are among many popular meals you can make at home, then freeze in containers and haul in the camping cooler. When on the road, buy fruit and vegetables from roadside stands. Picnic lunches at free rest stops beat the cost of eating out during the day and make for a nice break if you're road weary.

When eating out, look for breakfast specials (often served around the clock) and reduced-price luncheon menus. Some restaurants charge 25 to 50 percent more for lunch food, which they bill as supper fare, after four or five o'clock.

Car Camping Money Savers

Gasoline taxes vary widely from state to state. In 1991, for example, the fuel tax in Georgia was only 7 1/2 cents per gallon compared to 26 cents per gallon in Rhode Island. So if you're driving, it pays to know when and where to fill the gas tank. Stop by any AAA office and buy a copy of *Digest of Motor Laws* for $7.95, or call AAA at (407) 444-7962 for more information. In addition to listing state gasoline tax rates, the book summarizes towing requirements and other laws and regulations in the U.S. and Canada.

If the boat or camper you're towing is level with your vehicle, you will burn less gasoline. Adding a cab-flush topper to a pickup truck cuts down on wind drag and improves gas mileage. If you do not have a topper, drop the tailgate on the truck when traveling.

Other ways to add miles per gallon include keeping tires properly inflated, making sure your vehicle is correctly tuned, avoiding sudden stops and starts, and running the air conditioner only while the windows are up.

In mountainous country adjusting the air-intake screw on your vehicle's careburetor (if so equipped) will boost power and fuel economy. Avoid toll roads. Secondary highways and back roads are more interesting anyway.

Trip Tips

Travel by train, airplane, bus or boat can save time and money versus driving your own vehicle. Most domestic airlines allow two carry-ons and two pieces of checked luggage to seventy or more pounds total. That's more camping gear than I can comfortably carry. Sometimes bus companies offer unlimited travel promotions for a set fee during a prescribed period of time. A few years ago, crossing Lake Michigan by ferry saved my family and me 400 miles and eight hours of driving on a long camping trip. We pocketed about $50 in savings, too, and the kids enjoyed the diversion as much as my wife and I did.

Speaking of children, admission fees to amusement parks and sundry other tourist traps can be shockingly expensive. Free or low-cost activities include public museums and historical houses, government offices, factory and farm tours. Instead of wasting money on costly souvenirs, encourage the kids to collect natural treasures like rocks and seashells.

CAMPING FOR DISABLED PEOPLE

An estimated 43 million Americans have some form of disability. As our population ages and lives longer, the number of people with various disabilities is increasing. Mobility-impaired people in particular often have difficulty camping. Beaches are off-limits for wheelchair-users because the chairs spin out in the sand. Restroom doors may be too heavy to open alone. Wheeling down asphalt trails that have a crown in the middle gives them a sore back. Trails with more than a five percent grade can't be easily negotiated by someone on crutches.

The Universal Access Design Concept

Despite these and other hurdles, help is on the way for disabled campers. Sweeping the country is a concept called "universal access," new words perhaps but with the force of federal law behind them. The 1990 Americans with Disabilities Act (ADA) requires government agencies at all levels, as well as certain private and commercial enterprises, to provide equal access to everyone regardless of physical impairment. This includes outdoor recreation at the nation's campgrounds ranging from modern urban parks to rustic wilderness sites.

Some say the new law is the most sweeping social legislation passed since the 1964 Civil Rights Act. The ADA is rapidly changing how campers access the outdoors, as well as what facilities look like.

The law has caught many off guard, and there is confusion on how it will be implemented. Until the Forest Service came out with its new handbook, *Design Guide for Universal Access to Outdoor Recreation,* no one could agree, for example, what constitutes a fully accessible fishing dock or campsite. It is rapidly becoming the textbook of standards.

And some day entire campgrounds will be fully accessible, not just one of every twenty campsites. Toilets, showers and other support facilities, for instance, will be located closer to the people they serve. Connecting trails will be hard-surfaced and wide enough to permit people in wheelchairs to pass each other.

The universal or "whole access" design concept requires campsites to be located on fairly level terrain and to provide a large, hard-surfaced pad to house a picnic table, grill, electrical outlet and parking space for the camper or vehicle. Under old guidelines of the Architectural and Transportation Barriers Compliance Board, tent pads must be flat, stable, at least 17 feet by 20 feet in size, and located next to the hard-surfaced area. Tree branches have to be pruned to a height of at least 80 inches, and other dangerous obstructions removed.

Picnic tables are considered accessible to wheelchair-bound campers when the top of the table extends past the legs at least 19 inches on both ends, and there is a minimum of 29 inches of space between the underside of the top and the ground. Many newer tables provide spacing between the long seats so disabled campers don't always have to sit on the ends.

There must be at least 4 feet of clearance around picnic tables and grills, which should swivel to accommodate wind direction and feature cooking surfaces that are 30 to 36 inches high. These are a few of the many guidelines the USFS, which estimates that 19.2 million Americans are unable to walk farther than a quarter-mile, has reviewed.

Able-bodied campers don't realize how hard it is for someone with a mobility impairment to get a drink of water from a fountain or how dangerous it is to cook over a ground-level fireplace when you're leaning over from a wheelchair. Even hard-surfaced trails with vertical joints or edges higher than a quarter-inch can be tough for someone in a wheelchair to use. Crushed stone or pea rock that looks nice for trail bedding becomes a nightmare to someone trying to plow through the loose, catching material on crutches or in a wheelchair.

Most older campgrounds can be retrofitted to make them fully accessible, but the process may be expensive, and most states do not have the resources although all states have been required to prepare an action plan. However, when universal access is incorporated into the design of *new* public facilities (also mandated by the ADA), the additional cost is only about one percent.

Other changes are occurring. While some campers with disabilities want the security and comfort of a developed campground, others seek more challenging activities. This includes access to wilderness. According to the USFS, at least 15 outfitters now specialize in serving disabled people, an estimated 10,000 to 50,000 of whom visit semi-primitive and primitive areas each year. A recent survey of 80 such persons showed that only 5 percent had used motorized vehicles for getting into wilderness. Seventy-one percent relied on canoes. Hiking (39 percent), kayaking (29 percent), rafting (29 percent), horses (21 percent) and dogsled (19 percent) were other means of transportation. Half of the respondents also relied on their manual wheelchairs.

New products such as tents that set up simply, quickly and self-igniting stoves and lanterns are helping disabled campers to better enjoy the outdoors. Further, many manufacturers of travel trailers and other RVs are incorporating the whole access concept into the design of their units. Floor-mounted lifts are available as optional equipment in some RVs. The new Coleman Evergreen folding camping trailer from Fleetwood is purposely open and spacious and comes with a custom-designed tub and shower and a low-profile sink. An optional 64-by-40-inch platform with ramp for wheelchair access is available.

More news: The Bureau of Reclamation is designing the nation's first computerized program for instant information on accessibility. By the time you read this, campers will be able to dial a toll-free number to call Accessibility Data Management System (ADMS) and plan a trip anywhere in the country. At first ADMS will tie together those federal agencies offering public recreation. Later, state, local and perhaps even private campgrounds will join the partnership.

Regardless of our physical condition, these are exciting and challenging times for those of us who love to camp.

APPENDIX

MANUFACTURERS OF CAMPING EQUIPMENT

TENTS, SLEEPING BAGS, SLEEPING PADS AND PACKS

American Camper
14760 Santa Fe Trail Dr.
Lenexa, KS 66215
(913) 492-3200
(tents and packs)

Bibler Tents
5441 Western Ave.
Boulder, CO 80301
(303) 449-7351
(tents)

Black Diamond Equipment Ltd.
P.O. Box 110
Ventura, CA 93002
(805) 650-1395
(tents and backpacks)

Blue Ridge Pads
Foam Design Consumer Products, Inc.
Box 11184
(606) 231-7006
(sleeping pads)

Camel Outdoor Products
5988 Peachtree Corners East
Norcross, GA 30071
(404) 449-4689
(tents and accessories)

Canvas Cabins
35935 S.E. Bowman Rd.
Estacada, OR 97023
(503) 630-5000
(wall tents)

Caribou Mountaineering
P.O. Box 3696
Chico, CA 95927
(916) 891-6415
(sleeping bags and packs)

Cascade Designs
4000 1st Ave. S.
Seattle, WA 98134
(106) 583-0583
(sleeping pads and dry bags)

Cloud 9
P.O. Drawer G
Haleyville, AL 35565
(800) 221-7452
(sleeping bags)

The Coleman Co.
250 St. Francis St.
Wichita, KS 67201
(316) 261-3211
(tents, packs and sleeping bags)

The Colorado Tent Co.
222 Blake St.
Denver, CO 80205-2097
(303) 294-0924
(wall tents)

Dana Design
1950 N. 19th St.
Bozeman, MT 59715
(406) 587-4188
(backpacks)

Diamond Brand Canvas
Hwy. 25
Naples, NC 28760
(704) 684-9848
(tents)

Eastern Mountain Sports
One Vose Farm Rd.
Peterborough, NH 03458
(603) 924-6154
(sleeping bags)

Eastpak
50 Rogers Rd.
Ward Hill, MA 01835
(508) 373-1581
(packs)

Ellington Rucksack
0112 S.W. Hamilton
Portland, OR 97201

(503) 223-7457
(leather packs)

Envirogear
127 Elm St.
Cortland, NY 13045
(607) 753-8801
(sleeping bags)

Feathered Friends
2013 4th Ave.
Seattle, WA 98121
(206) 324-4166
(sleeping bags)

Foam Design
444 Transport Ct.
Lexington, KY 40509
(606) 231-7006
(sleeping pads)

Frelonic
P.O. Box 169
Salem, MA 01970
(508) 744-0300
(sleeping pads)

Gold-Eck of Austria
6313 Seaview Ave. N.W.
Seattle, WA 98107
(206)781-0886
(sleeping bags)

Goode Products, Inc.
2801 E. 12th St.
Los Angeles, CA 90023
(213) 269-1183
(sleeping products)

Granite Gear
P.O. Box 278
Two Harbors, MN 55616
(218) 834-6157
(packs)

Gregory Mountain Products
100 Calle Cortez
Temucula, CA 92390
(800) 477-3420
(backpacks)

Gymwell Corp.
23555 Telo Ave.
Torrance, CA 90505
(800) 466-6856
(sleeping pads)

High Country Outdoor Products
19991 S.E. Foster Rd.
Boring, OR 97009
(503) 658-4704
(inflatable mats)

Integral Designs
5516 Third St. S.E.
Calgary, Alberta
Canada T2H lJ9
(403) 640-1445
(sleeping bags)

Jansport
10411 Airport Rd. S.W.
Everett, WA 78204
(206) 743-0300
(backpacks)

JWA Camping Division
P.O. Box 966
Binghamton, NY 13902-0966
(607) 723-7546
(Eureka! tents, Camp
   Trails backpacks)

Kelty Pack
P.O. Box 7048-A
St. Louis, MO 63177
(314) 576-8005
(backpacks)

Lafuma U.S.A.
P.O. Box 812
Farmington, GA 30638
(706) 769-6627
(packs)

Lone Peak Designs
3474 South 2300 East
Salt Lake City, UT 84109
(801) 272-5217
(packs)

Lowe Alpine Systems
P.O. Box 1449
Broomfield, CO 80038
(303) 465-0522
(backpacks)

Madden
2400 Central
Boulder, CO 80301
(303) 442-5828
(packs)

Mark Pack Works
230 Madison St.
Oakland, CA 94607
(510) 452-0243
(packs)

**Marmot Mountain
   International**
2321 Circadian Way
Santa Rosa, CA 95407
(707) 544-4590
(sleeping bags)

Montana Canvas
Box 390
Belgrade, MT 59714
(406) 388-1225
(wall tents)

Montbell America
245 M Mount Herman Rd.,
   Ste. A
Scotts Valley, CA 95066
(408) 476-2400
(sleeping bags, backpacks)

Moonstone Mountaineering
5350 Ericson Way
Arcata, CA 95521
(707) 822-2985
(sleeping bags)

Moss Tentworks
P.O. Box 309
Camden, ME 04843
(207) 236-8368
(tents)

Mountain Cat
P.O. Box 32
Normantown, WV 25267
(304) 462-7755
(wall tents)

Mountain Equipment
4776 E. Jensen
Fresno, CA 93725
(209) 486-8211
(backpacks)

Mountainsmith
Heritage Square, Bldg. P
Golden, CO 80401
(303) 279-5930
(tents and backpacks)

MZH Sleeping Bags
80 East Route 4
Paramus, NJ 07652
(201) 909-0777
(sleeping bags)

Natural Balance Design
P.O. Box 1573

Fairfield, IA 52556
(515) 472-7918
(backpacks)

Nelson/Weather-Rite
14760 Santa Fe Trail Dr.
Lenexa, KS 66215
(913) 492-3200
(tents and packs)

Noall Tents
59530 Devils Ladder Rd.
Mountain Center, CA 92561
(909) 659-4219
(tents)

Northern Lights, Inc.
P.O. Box 3413
Mammoth Lakes, CA 93546
(619) 924-3833
(sleeping bags)

Osprey Packs
504 Central Ave.
Dolores, CO 81323
(303) 882-2221
(packs)

Outbound
1580 Zephyr Ave.
Hayward, CA 94545-6148
(800) 866-9880
(tents, packs)

Outdoor Recreation Group
533 S. Los Angeles St.
Los Angeles, CA 90013
(packs)

Overland Equipment
2145 Park Ave., #4
Chico, CA 95928
(916) 894-5605
(packs)

Pop Tent
1221 Brickell Ave., Ste. 1720
Miami, FL 33131
(305) 577-0020
(tents)

Premier International, Inc.
901 N. Stuart St., Ste. 804
Arlington, VA 22203
(703) 524-6464
(backpacks)

Quest
569 Charcot Ave.
San Jose, CA 95131
(800) 875-6901
(backpacks and tents)

Salem Tent & Awning Co.
280 Wallace Rd.,
NW Salem, OR 97304
(503) 363-4788
(wall tents)

San Antonio Tent
P.O. Box 200426
San Antonio, TX 78220
(512) 337-4142
(tents)

Sierra Designs
2039 4th St.
Berkley, CA 94710
(510) 843-0923
(tents and sleeping bags)

Slumberjack
1224 Fern Ridge Pkwy.
St. Louis, MO 63141
(314) 576-8000
(sleeping bags)

Softsports, Inc.
Rt. 4, Box 340
Elkton, VA 22827

(703) 289-9685.
(pop tents)

Superior Packs
3838 Dight Ave. S.
Minneapolis, MN 55406
(612) 721-5785
(packs)

The North Face
999 Harrison St.
Berkley, CA 94710
(510) 527-9700
(tents and backpacks)

Tough Traveler
1012 State St.
Schenectady, NY 12307
(518) 377-8526
(packs)

VauDe
P.O. Box 3413
Mammoth Lakes, CA 93546
(619) 924-3833
(packs)

Vortex
548 West 9320 South
Salt Lake City, UT 84070
(801) 568-1825
(packs)

Walrus
620 Compton
Broomfield, CO 80038
(303) 465-3707
(tents)

Wenzel
1224 Fern Ridge Parkway
St. Louis, MO 63141
(800) 325-4121
(tents and sleeping bags)

Western Mountain Sports
1025 S. 5th
San Jose, CA 95112
(408) 287-8944
(sleeping bags)

Wilderness Experience
20727 Dearborn St.
Chatsworth, CA 91311
(818) 341-5774
(backpacks)

Winnebago (Avid Outdoor)
P.O. Box 578
Olathe, KS 66051-0578
(913) 780-2843
(tents)

Woods Canada
401 Logan Ave.
Toronto, Ontario
Canada M4M 2P2
(416) 465-2403
(sleeping bags and packs)

LANTERNS AND LIGHTS, STOVES AND COOKWARE

Alco-Brite
685 Hilldale St.
Hilldale, UT 84784-0926
(801) 874-1025
(stoves)

Athena/Aervoe-Pacific Co., Inc.
1198 Sawmill Rd.
Gardnerville, NV 89410
(800) 227-0196
(stoves)

Brightwell Enterprises
8816 Manchester Rd., Ste. 200
Brentwood, MO 63144
(solar rechargeable lantern)

Brinkmann Corp.
4215 McEwen
Dallas, TX 75244
(214) 387-4939
(lights)

Camp Chef
675 North 600 West
Logan, UT 84321
(801) 752-3922
(stoves and accessories)

Camping Gaz/Suunto U.S.A.
2151 Las Palmas Dr., Ste. G
Carlsbad, CA 92009
(619) 931-6788
(stoves and fuel)

Century Primus
P.O. Box 188
Cherry Valley, IL 60106
(815) 332-4951
(propane stoves and lanterns)

The Coleman Co.
250 St. Francis St.
Wichita, KS 67201
(316) 261-3211
(stoves, lanterns, heaters,
    fuel and cookware)

Epigas/Taymar
2755 S. 160th St.
New Berlin, WI 53151-3601
(414) 821-8180
(stoves and fuel)

Foldin-Cooker
P.O. Box 157445
Irving, TX 75015
(214) 579-7515
(camping grill)

Fox Hill Corp.
P.O. Box 259
Rozet, WY 82727
(307) 682-5358
(Sportsman's and Outfitter's
    portable ovens)

GSI Sports
7949 Stromesa Ct., Ste. X
San Diego, CA 92126
(619) 271-7816
(cookware)

Lodge Cast Iron Manufacturing
P.O. Box 380
South Pittsburg, TN 37380
(515) 837-7181
(Dutch ovens and other
    cast iron cookware)

MSR
P.O. Box 24547
Seattle, WA 98124
(800) 877-9677
(stoves)

Mag Instrument
1635 S. Sacramento Ave.
Ontario, CA 91761
(714) 947-1006
(flashlights)

Markill/Bergsport Int.
P.O. Box 1519
Nederland, CO 80466
(303) 258-3796
(stoves)

Metal Ware Corp.
1710 Monroe St.
Two Rivers, WI 54241
(414) 793-1368
(Open Country cookware)

Mr. Camper Products, Inc.
P.O. Box 6660
Cleveland, OH 44101
(800) 251-0001
(propane stoves, lanterns and
    heaters)

Paulin Products, Inc.
4780 Beidler Rd.
Willoughby, OH 44094
(800) 272-8546
(propane lanterns)

G. T. Price Products, Inc.
2320 E. Valencia Dr.
Fullerton, CA 92631-4904
(714) 525-5483
(flashlights)

Streamlight
1030 W. Germantown Park
Norristown, PA 19403
(215) 631-0600
(flashlights)

Tekna
1500 Klondike Rd. S.W.
Conyers, GA 30207
(404) 922-1632
(flashlights)

Traveling Light
836 Santa Fe Ave.
Albany, CA 94706
(415) 526-8401
(camping ovens)

ZZ Corp.
10806 Kaylor St.
Los Alamitos, CA 90720
(310) 598-3220
(stoves)

COOLERS

Airlite Plastics Company
914 North 18th Street
Omaha, NE 68102
(402) 341-7300

The Coleman Company, Inc.
250 North St. Francis
Wichita, KS 67202
(316) 261-3211

Igloo Products Corp.
P.O. Box 19322
Houston, TX 77224-9322
(713) 465-2571

Plastilite Corp.
P.O. Box 12347
Omaha, NE 68112
(402) 453-7500

Rubbermaid, Inc.
Specialty Products Div.
Wooster, OH 44691
(216) 264-6464

The Thermos Company
Route 75 East
Freeport, IL 61032
(800) 243-0745

CAMP STOOLS, TABLES, COTS

Byer Manufacturing
P.O. Box 100
Orono, ME 04473
(207) 866-2171

Crazy Creek Products
1401 S. Broadway

Red Lodge, MT 59068
(406) 446-3446

Sierra
P.O. Box 806
Fort Smith, AR 72902
(918) 436-7701

WATER FILTERS

Katadyn
3020 N. Scottsdale Rd.
Scottsdale, AZ 85251
(602) 990-3131

Pur
2229 Edgewood Ave. S.
Minneapolis, MN 55426
(612) 541-1313

Relags U.S.A.
14 Weaver Dr.
Boulder, CO 80302
(303) 440-8047

SweetWater
4725 Nautilus Ct. S.
Boulder, CO 80301
(303) 530-2715

WTC Industries
14405 21st Ave. N., #120
Plymouth, MN 55447
(612) 473-1625

COMPASSES

Buck Knives, Inc.
Box 1267
El Cajon, CA 92022
(800) 326-2825

Brunton U.S.A.
620 East Monroe
Riverton, WY 82501
(307) 856-6559

Compass Industries, Inc.
104 East 25th St.
New York, NY 10010
(800) 221-9904

Silva Compasses
Box 966
Binghamton, NY 13902
(800) 847-1460

Selsi Co., Inc.
40 Veterans Blvd.
Carlstadt, NJ 07072-0497
(800) ASK SELSI

Suunto U.S.A.
2151-F Las Palmas Dr.
Carlsbad, CA 92009
(616) 931-6788

CAMPING ACCESSORIES

Basic Designs
335-A O'Hair Ct.
Santa Rosa, CA 95407
(707) 575-1220

Coghlans Ltd.
121 Irene St.
Winnipeg, Manitoba
Canada R3T 4C7
(204) 284-9550

E-Z Camping
P.O. Box 831343
San Antonio, TX 78283
(210) 227-9113

Kenyon Consumer Products
P.O. Box 3715
Peace Dale, RI 02883
(401) 792-3704

Liston Concepts
2550 South 2300 West, Ste. 1
Salt Lake City, UT 84119
(801) 972-8282

LMG Reliance
1093 Sherwin Rd.
Winnipeg, Manitoba
Canada R3H lA4
(204) 633-4403

MPI Outdoor Safety Products
37 East St.
Winchester, MA 01890-1198
(800) 343-5827

Northwest River Supplies
2009 S. Main
Moscow, ID 83843
(208) 883-4787

Safesport Manufacturing Co.
1100 W. 45th Ave.
Denver, CO 80211
(303) 433-6506

Texsport
Box 55326
Houston, TX 77255-5326
(800) 231-1402

Voyageurs
P.O. Box 207
Waitsfield, VT 05673
(802) 496-6247

MISCELLANEOUS

Atwater Carey Ltd.
218 Gold Run Rd.
Boulder, CO 80302
(303) 444-9326
(first aid kits)

B.C.B. Survival Equipment
7907 N.W. 53rd St. #310
Miami, FL 33166
(305) 594-9242
(first aid kits)

Dawn Marketing, Inc.
474 Genesee St.
Avon, NY 14414
(800) 724-3529
(Sawvivor camp saw)

Garcia Machine
14097 Ave. 272
Visalia, CA 93277
(209) 732-3785
(bear-resistant food containers)

Gerber Legendary Blades
14200 S.W. 72nd Ave.
Portland, OR 97223
(503) 639-6161
(knives, camping tools)

Man of Rubber
Rt. 1, Box 93-B
Reliance, TN 37369
(800) 437-9224
(dry bags)

Nalgene
215 Tremont
Rochester, NY 14608
(water bottles)

Nuwick
P.O. Box 7962
Van Nuys, CA 91409
(310) 396-3135
(survival candles)

Pelican Products
2255 Jefferson St.
Torrance, CA 90501
(dry boxes)

Sawyer Products
P.O. Box 188
Safety Harbor, FL 34695
(813) 725-1177
(first-aid kits)

MAJOR RETAILERS AND MAIL ORDER HOUSES

Bass Pro Shops
1935 S. Campbell
Springfield, MO 65898-0300
(800) 227-7776

Bike Nashbar
4111 Simon Rd.
Youngstown, OH 44512
(800) 627-4227

Cabela's
812 - 13th Ave.
Sidney, NE 69160
(800) 237-4444

Campmor
P.O. Box 997
Paramus, NJ 07652
(800) 526-4784

Gander Mountain, Inc.
P.O. Box 248
Wilmot, WI 53192
(800) 558-9410

Don Gleason's
Campers Supply, Inc.
413 Pearl Street
Northampton, MA 01061

Indiana Camp Supply, Inc.
P.O. Box 2166
Loveland, CO 80539
(303) 669-8884

L.L. Bean
Freeport, ME 04033
(800) 221-4221

Le Baron Outdoor
Products, Ltd.
8601 St-Laurent Blvd.
Montreal, Quebec
Canada H2P 2M9
(514) 381-4231

Leisure Outlet Discount
Camping Equipment
421 Soquel Ave.
Santa Cruz, CA 95062
(800) 322-1460

REI
Sumner, WA 98352-0001)
(800) 426-4840

Sierra Trading Post
5025 Campstool Rd.
Cheyenne, WY 82007
(307) 775-8000

CAMPING ORGANIZATIONS

American Canoe Association
7432 Alban Station Blvd.
Ste. B-226
Springfield, VA 22150
(703) 451-0141

American Hiking Society
P.O. Box 20160
Washington, DC 20041
(703) 385-3252

Good Sam Club (RV owners)
P.O. Box 6060
Camarillo, CA 93011
(805) 389-0300

Museum of Family Camping
100 Athol Rd.
Richmond, NH 03470
(603) 239-4768

National Outdoor Leadership
School (NOLS)
P.O. Box AA
Lander, WY 82520
(307) 332-6973

North American
Paddlesports Assn.
12455 N. Wauwatosa Rd.
McQuon, WI 53092
(414) 242-5228

Outdoors Forever
P.O. Box 4832
East Lansing, MI 48823
(517) 337-0018
(advocacy group for disabled people)

RV Elderhostel
75 Federal St.
Boston, MA 02110-1941
(617) 426-7788

RVing Women
21413 W. Lost Lake Rd.
Snohomish, WA 98290
(800) 333-9992

RECOMMENDED READING

MAGAZINES

Backpacking	*Motorhome*	*Disabled*
Bicycling	*Outdoor Life*	*Outdoors Magazine*
Canoe & Kayak	*Outside*	2052 W. 23rd St.
Chevy Outdoors	*Trailer Life*	Chicago, IL 60608
Field & Stream	*Sports Afield*	(708) 358–4160

BOOKS

America's Secret Recreation Areas by Michael Hodgson. Foghorn Press, 1993.

Backpacking by Joel F. Meier. Sagamore Publishing, second edition, 1993.

Backpacking in the 90's by Victoria Logue. Menasha Ridge Press, l993.

Backpacking with Babies and Small Children by Goldie Silverman. Wilderness Press, Second Edition, 1986.

The Basic Essentials of Edible Wild Plants and Useful Herbs by Jim Meuninck. ICS Books, 1988.

The Book of Outdoor Knots by Peter Owen. Lyons & Burford, 1993

Camp and Trail Cooking Techniques by Jim Capossela. The Countryman Press, Inc., 1994.

Camping's Forgotten Skills by Cliff Jacobson. ICS Books, 1993.

Camping for Kids by Stephen and Elizabeth Griffin. NorthWord Press, 1994.

Camping with Kids by Don Wright. Cottage Publications, Inc., 1992.

Canoe Country Camping: Wilderness Skills for the Boundary Waters and Quetico by Michael Furtman. Pfeifer-Hamilton, 1992.

Cold Comfort by Glenn Randall. Lyons & Burford, 1987.

Complete Outdoors Encyclopedia by Vin T. Sparano. Outdoor Life Books, revised and expanded, 1988.

The Cross Country Primer by Laurie Gullion. Lyons & Burford, 1990.

Desert Hiking by Dave Ganci. Wilderness Press, 1994.

Don Wright's Guide to Free Campgrounds by Don Wright. Cottage Publications, Inc., 1990.

Don Wright's Save-A-Buck Camping by Don Wright. Cottage Publications, Inc., 1991.

Emergency Medical Procedures for the Outdoors by Patient Medical Associates. Menasha Ridge Press, 1992.

The Family Canoe Trip by Carl Shepardson. ICS Books, 1985

A Guide to Backpacking with Your Dog by Charlene G. LaBelle. Alpine Publications, 1993.

Harsh Weather Camping in the '90s by Sam Curtis. Menasha Ridge Press, 1993.

Knots for Hikers & Backpackers by Frank Logue with Victoria Logue. Menasha Ridge Press (1994)

The L. L. Bean Guide to the Outdoors by Bill Riviere with the staff of L. L. Bean. Random House, 1981.

The Modern Backpacker's Handbook: An Environmental Guide by Glenn Randall. Lyons & Burford, 1994.

Mountaineering: The Freedom of the Hills, written and The Mountaineers, 1993.

The New Complete Walker III by Colin Fletcher. Alfred A. Knopf, 1986.

The Outward Bound Wilderness First-Aid Handbook by Jeff Isaac and Peter Goth, M.D. Published by Lyons & Burford, 1991.

Sea Kayaking Basics by David Harrison. William Morrow & Co., 1994.

Simple Foods for the Pack by Claudia Axcell, Diana Cooke, and Vikki Kinmont. Sierra Club Books, 1986.

Standard First Aid & Personal Safety. the American Red Cross,
    Second Edition, 1979.
The U.S. Outdoor Atlas & Recreation Guide by John Oliver Jones.
    Houghton Mifflin, 1992.
Wilderness with Children by Michael Hodgson. Stackpole Books, 1992.
Wilderness Ranger Cookbook, A Collection of Backcountry Recipes by
    Forest Service Wilderness Rangers. Falcon Press, 1990.
Woodall's Campground Directories. Woodall Publishing Co., 28167
    North Keith Dr., Lake Forest, IL 60045 (revised annually).

FEDERAL, STATE AND PROVINCIAL AGENCIES

FEDERAL AGENCIES

Camping opportunities are available on many federally managed public lands. The federal agencies staff regional and sometimes district offices, too. For more information, contact these national headquarters.

Bureau of Land Management
Div. of Recreation and Wilderness
  Resources
1849 C Street N.W.
Washington, D.C. 20240
(202) 658-8828

Bureau of Reclamation
Pacific Northwest Region
Box 043
550 W. Fort St.
Boise, ID 83724
(208) 334-9680

National Park Service
P.O. Box 37127
Washington, D.C. 20013
(202) 343-4747
(800)- 452-111
  (for campground reservations)

U.S. Army Corps of Engineers
Regional Brochures, IM-MV-N
3909 Halls Ferry Rd.
Vicksburg, MS 39180-6199

U.S. Fish & Wildlife Service
1849 C St. N.W., Room 3245
Washington, D.C. 20240
(202) 343-4311

U.S. Forest Service
Box 96090
Washington, D.C. 20090
(202) 205-1760
(800) 283-CAMP (for campground reservations)

STATE AGENCIES

Each state's natural resources or game and fish department is broken into many divisions. Camping opportunities usually fall under the management of the forests, parks or recreation divisions. If you are unsure, ask first for the public affairs department (sometimes called the information and education department).

State travel bureaus are another good source of camping information and can often direct you to regional, county or local chambers of commerce and other groups that can help.

ALABAMA

**Dept. of Conservation
and Natural Resources**
64 N. Union St.
Montgomery, AL 36130
(205) 242-3486

Bureau of Tourism and Travel
P.O. Box 4309
Montgomery, AL 36103-4309
(205) 242-4169
(800)-ALABAMA

ALASKA

Dept. of Natural Resources
400 Willoughby, 5th Floor
Juneau, AK 99801
(907) 465-2400

Division of Tourism P.O.
Box 110801

Juneau, AK 99811-0801
(907) 465-2010

ARIZONA

Game and Fish Department
2221 W. Greenway Rd.
Phoenix, AZ 85023
(602) 942-3000

Office of Tourism
1100 W. Washington
Phoenix, AZ 85007
(602) 542-8687

ARKANSAS

Game and Fish Commission
#2 Natural Resources Dr.
Little Rock, AR 72205
(501) 223-6300

Dept. of Parks and Tourism
One Capitol Mall
Little Rock, AR 72201
(501) 682-7777
(800) NATURAL

CALIFORNIA

Dept. of Parks and Recreation
P.O. Box 942896
Sacramento, CA 94296-0001
(916) 445-2358

Office of Tourism
P.O. Box 9278
Van Nuys, CA 91409
(916) 322-2881
(800) TO-CALIF

COLORADO

Dept. of Natural Resources
1313 Sherman, Room 718
Denver, CO 80203
(303) 866-3311

Tourism Board
P.O. Box 38700
Denver, CO 80238
(303) 592-5410
(800) COLORADO

CONNECTICUT

**Dept. of Environmental
Protection**
165 Capitol Ave.
Hartford, CT 06106
(203) 566-4683

**Dept. of Economic
Development**
Tourism Division
865 Brook St.
Rocky Hill, CT 06067
(800) CT-BOUND

DELAWARE

**Dept. of Natural Resources and
Environmental Control**
P.O. Box 1401
Dover, DE 19903
(302) 739-5295

Tourism Office
Box 1401
Dover, DE 19903
(302) 739-4271
(800) 441-884

FLORIDA

Dept. of Natural Resources
3900 Commonwealth Blvd.
Tallahassee, FL 32399-3000
(904) 488-1554

Div. of Tourism
126 W. Van Buren St.
Tallahassee, FL 32301
(904) 487-1462

GEORGIA

Dept. of Natural Resources
205 Butler St. SE
Atlanta, GA 30334
(404) 656-3522

**Dept. of Industry, Trade &
Tourism**
P.O. Box 1776
Atlanta, GA 30301
(404) 656-3590
(800) VISIT-GA

HAWAII

**Dept. of Land and
Natural Resources**
Box 621
Honolulu, HI 96809
(808) 587-0400

**Dept. of Business, Economic
Development & Tourism**
P.O. Box 2359
Honolulu, HI 96804
(808) 586-2423

IDAHO

Fish and Game Department
Box 25
Boise, ID 83707
(208) 334-3700

Div. of Tourism Development
700 W. State St., Dept. C
Boise, ID 83720
(208) 334-2470
(800) 635-7820

ILLINOIS

Dept. of Conservation
524 S. Second St.
Springfield, IL 62701-1787
(217) 782-6302

Bureau of Tourism
100 W. Randolph, Ste. 3-400
Chicago, IL 60601
 (312) 814-4732
(800) 635-7820

INDIANA

Dept. of Natural Resources
402 W. Washington St., #C256
Indianapolis, IN 46204-2212
(317) 232-4080

Dept. of Commerce
 and Tourism
One North Capitol, Ste. 700
Indianapolis, IN 46204-2288
(317) 232-8860
(800) 289-6646

IOWA

Dept. of Natural Resources
E. Ninth and Grand Ave.
Des Moines, IA 50319-0034
(515) 281-5145

Div. of Tourism
200 East Grand
Des Moines, IA 50309
(515) 242-4705
(800) 345-IOWA

KANSAS

Dept. of Wildlife and Parks
900 Jackson St., Ste. 502
Topeka, KS 66612-1220
(913) 296-2281

Travel and Tourism Div.
400 W. 8th St., 5th Floor
Topeka, KS 66603-3957
(913) 296-3009
(800) 252-6727

KENTUCKY

Dept. of Fish and
 Wildlife Resources
#1 Game Farm Rd.
Frankfort, KY 40601
(502) 564-3400

Dept. of Travel Development
2200 Capitol Plaza Tower
Frankfort, KY 40601
(502) 564-4930
(800) 225-TRIP

LOUISIANA

Dept. of Wildlife and Fisheries
P.O. Box 98000
Baton Rouge, LA 70898-9000
(504) 765-2800

Office of Tourism
P.O. Box 94291
Baton Rouge, LA 70804-9291
(504) 342-8119
(800) 33-GUMBO

MAINE

Dept. of Conservation
State House Station #22
Augusta, ME 04333
(207) 289-2211

Office of Tourism
189 State St.
Augusta, ME 04333
(207) 289-5711
(800) 533-9595

MARYLAND

Dept. of Natural Resources
Tawes State Office Bldg.
Annapolis, MD 21401
(301) 974-3195

Office of Tourism Development
217 E. Redwood St., 9th Floor
Baltimore, MD 21202
(410) 333-6611
(800) 543-1036

MASSACHUSETTS

**Division of Fisheries
and Wildlife**
100 Cambridge St.
Boston, MA 02202
(617) 727-2864

Office of Travel and Tourism
100 Cambridge St., 13th Floor
Boston, MA 02202
(617) 727-3201

MICHIGAN

Dept. of Natural Resources
P.O. Box 30028
Lansing, MI 48909
(517) 373-1214

Travel Bureau
P.O. Box 30226
Lansing, MI 48909
(517) 373-0670
(800) 5432-YES

MINNESOTA

Dept. of Natural Resources
500 Lafayette Rd.
St. Paul, MN 55155-4001
(612) 296-6157

Office of Tourism
375 Jackson St.
St. Paul, MN 55101
(612) 296-5029
(800) 657-3700

MISSISSIPPI

Dept. of Wildlife,
    Fisheries and Parks
P.O. Box 451
Jackson, MS 39205
(601) 362-9212

Div. of Tourism
P.O. Box 22825
Jackson, MS 39205
(601) 395-3297
(800) 647-2290

MISSOURI

Department of Conservation
P.O. Box 180
Jefferson City, MO 65102-0180
(314) 751-4115

Div. of Tourism
P.O. Box 1055
Jefferson City, MO 65102
(314) 751-4133
(800) 877-1234

MONTANA

Dept. of Natural Resources
    and Conservation
1520 East Sixth Ave.
Helena, MT 59620-2301
(406) 444-6699

Travel Montana
Room 259
Deer Lodge, MT 59722
(406) 444-2654
(800) 541-1447

NEBRASKA

Game and Parks Commission
P.O. Box 30370
Lincoln, NE 68503
(402) 471-0641

Div. of Travel and Tourism
301 Centennial Mall S.
    Room 88937
Lincoln, NE 68509
(402) 471-3796
(800) 223-4307

NEVADA

Dept. of Conservation
    and Natural Resources
123 W. Nye Ln.
Carson City, NV 89710
(702) 687-4360

Commission of Tourism
Capitol Complex
Carson City, NV 89710
(702) 687-4322
(800) NEVADA-8

NEW HAMPSHIRE

Fish and Game Dept.
2 Hazen Dr.
Concord, NH 03301
(603) 271-3421

Office of Travel and Tourism
P.O. Box 856
Concord, NH 03302
(603) 271-2343

NEW JERSEY

Div. of Parks and Forestry
401 East State St., CN 404
Trenton, NJ 08625-0402
(609) 292-2733

Div. of Travel and Tourism
20 West State St., CN 826
Trenton, NJ 08625
(609) 292-2470
(800) JERSEY-7

NEW MEXICO

Dept. of Fish and Game
P.O. Box 25112
Santa Fe, NM 87504
(505) 827-2911

Dept. of Tourism
1100 St. Francis Dr.
Santa Fe, NM 87503
(505) 827-0291
(800) 545-2040

NEW YORK

**Dept. of Environmental
  Conservation**
50 Wolf Rd.
Albany, NY 12233
(518) 457-5400

**Dept. of Economic
  Development**
One Commerce Plaza
Albany, NY 12245
(518) 474-4116
(800) CALL-NYS

NORTH CAROLINA

Wildlife Resources Commission
512 N. Salisbury St.
Raleigh, NC 27604-1188
(919) 733-3391

Div. of Travel and Tourism
430 N. Salisbury St.
Raleigh, NC 27603
(919) 733-4171
(800) VISIT-NC

NORTH DAKOTA

Game and Fish Dept.
100 N. Bismarck Expressway
Bismarck, ND 58501
(701) 221-6300

Tourism Promotion
Liberty Memorial Bldg.
Bismarck, ND 58505
(701) 224-2525
(800) HELLO-ND

OHIO

Dept. of Natural Resources
Fountain Square
Columbus, OH 43224
(614) 265-6565

Div. of Travel and Tourism
P.O. Box 1001
Columbus, OH 43211-0101
(614) 466-8844
(800) BUCKEYE

OKLAHOMA

Dept. of Wildlife Conservation
P.O. Box 53465
Oklahoma City, OK 73152
(405) 521-3851

Tourism & Recreation Dept.
Travel and Tourism Div.
500 Will Rogers Bldg., DA92
Oklahoma City
  OK 73105-4492
(405) 521-3981
(800) 652-6552

OREGON

Dept. of Fish and Wildlife
P.O. Box 59
Portland, OR 97207
(503) 229-5400

Economic Development Dept.
Tourism Div.
775 Summer St. NE
Salem, OR 97310
(503) 373-1270
(800) 547-7842

PENNSYLVANIA

Dept. of Environmental Resources
P.O. Box 2063
Harrisburg, PA 17120
(717) 783-8303

Bureau of Travel Marketing
130 Commonwealth Dr.
Warrendale, PA 15086
(717) 787-5453
(800) VISIT-PA

RHODE ISLAND

Dept. of Environmental
  Management
9 Hayes St.
Providence, RI 02908
(401) 277-2774

Tourism Div.
7 Jackson Walkway
Providence, RI 02903
(401) 277-2601
(800) 556-2484

SOUTH CAROLINA

Wildlife and Marine
  Resources Dept.
P.O. Box 167
Columbia, SC 29202
(803) 734-3888

Div. of Tourism
Box 71, Room 902
Columbia, SC 29202
(803) 734-0235

SOUTH DAKOTA

Game, Fish and Parks Dept.
523 E. Capitol
Pierre, SD 578501-3182
(605) 773-3387

Dept. of Tourism
711 E. Wells Ave.
Pierre, SD 57501-3369
(605) 773-3301
(800) 843-1930

TENNESSEE

Wildlife Resources Agency
P.O. Box 40747
Nashville, TN 37204
(615) 781-6500

**Dept. of Tourism
Development**
P.O. Box 23170
Nashville, TN 37202
(615) 741-2158

TEXAS

Parks and Wildlife Dept.
4200 Smith School Rd.
Austin, TX 78744
(512) 389-4800

Dept. of Commerce
Tourism Div.
P.O. Box 12728
Austin, TX 78711-2728
(512) 462-9191
(800) 88-88-TEX

UTAH

**Div. of Parks and
Recreation**
1636 W. North Temple
Salt Lake City, UT 84116-3156
(801) 538-7220

Travel Council
Council Hall/Capitol Hill
Salt Lake City, UT 84114
(801) 538-1030

VERMONT

**Dept. of Forests, Parks
and Recreation**
Waterbury Complex, 10 South
Waterbury, VT 05677
(802) 244-8715

Travel Div.
134 State St.
Montpelier, VT 05602
(802) 828-3236

VIRGINIA

**Dept. of Conservation
and Recreation**
203 Governor St., Ste. 302
Richmond, VA 23219
(804) 786-2121

Virginia Tourism
1021 E. Cary St.
Richmond, VA 23219
(804) 786-4484
(800) VISIT-VA

WASHINGTON

Dept. of Natural Resources
P.O. Box 47001
Olympia, WA 98504-7001
(206) 902-1000

Tourism Development Div.
P.O. Box 42513
Olympia, WA 98504-2513
(206) 586-2088
(800) 544-1800

WEST VIRGINIA

Dept. of Natural Resources
1900 Kanawha Blvd. E.
Charleston, WV 25305
(304) 348-2754

Div. of Tourism & Parks
2101 Washington Street E.
Charleston, WV 25305
(304) 348-2286
(800) 225-5982

WISCONSIN

Dept. of Natural Resources
Box 7921
Madison, WI 53707
(608) 266-2621

Div. of Tourism
P.O. Box 7606
Madison, WI 53707
(608) 266-2161
(800) 372-2737 (in-state)
(800) 432-TRIP (out-of-state)

WYOMING

Game and Fish Dept.
5400 Bishop Blvd.
Cheyenne, WY 82006
(307) 777-4601

Div. of Tourism
I-25 at College Drive
Cheyenne, WY 82002
(307) 777-7777
(800) 225-5996

PROVINCIAL AGENCIES

ALBERTA

**Dept. of Forestry, Lands
and Wildlife**
9945-108 St.
Edmonton, Alberta
Canada T5K 2G6
(403) 427-6749

Travel Alberta
10025 Jasper Ave., 15th Floor
Edmonton, Alberta
Canada T5J 3Z3
(800) 661-8888

BRITISH COLUMBIA

Ministry of Environment
Parliament Bldgs.
Victoria, British Columbia
Canada V8V lX5
(604) 387-5429

**Ministry of Tourism
Recreation and Culture**
Parliament Bldgs.
Victoria, British Columbia
Canada V8V lX4
(800) 663-6000

MANITOBA

Dept. of Natural Resources
314 Legislative Bldg.
Winnipeg, Manitoba
Canada R3C 0V8
(204) 945-3730

Travel Manitoba, Dept. 6020
155 Carlton St., 7th Floor
Winnipeg, Manitoba
Canada R3C 3H8
(800) 665-0040

NEW BRUNSWICK

**Dept. of Natural Resources
and Energy**
P.O. Box 6000
Fredericton, New Brunswick
Canada E3B 5H1
(506) 453-2440

**Tourism, Recreation
and Heritage**
P.O. Box 12345
Fredericton, New Brunswick
Canada E3B 5C3
(800) 561-0123

NEWFOUNDLAND
AND LABRADOR

**Dept. of Tourism and
Culture, Wildlife Division**
P.O. Box 8700
St. John's, Newfoundland
Canada A1B 4J6
(709) 729-2817

**Dept. of Development
and Tourism**
P.O. Box 2016, Station A
St. John's, Newfoundland
Canada A1C 5R8
(800) 563-6353

NORTHWEST
TERRITORIES

Dept. of Renewable Resources
Government of the Northwest Territories
P.O. Box 1320
Yellow Knife,
Northwest Territories
Canada X1A 2L9
(403) 920-8716

Travel Arctic
Government of the Northwest Territories
Yellowknife,
Northwest Territories
Canada NWT X1A
(800) 661-0788

ONTARIO

Ministry of Natural Resources
Public Information Center
Parliament Bldg. Toronto, Ontario
Canada M7A 1W3
(416) 965-4251

**Ministry of Tourism
and Recreation**
Queen's Park
Toronto, Ontario
Canada M7A 2E5
(800) 268-3735

PRINCE EDWARD ISLAND

Dept. of the Environment
P.O. Box 2000
Charlottetown,
    Prince Edward Island
Canada ClA 7N8
(902) 368-4683

**Dept. of Tourism and
    Parks Visitor Services**
P.O. Box 940
Charlottetown,
    Prince Edward Island
Canada PEI ClA
(800) 561-0123

QUEBEC

**Dept. of Recreation,
    Fish and Game**
150 East, St.-Cyrille Blvd.
Quebec City, Quebec
Canada GlR 4Yl
(418) 643-3127

Tourisme Quebec
P.O. Box 20,000
Quebec City, Quebec
Canada GlK 7X2
(800) 443-7000

SASKATCHEWAN

Parks & Renewable Resources
3211 Albert St.
Regina, Saskatchewan
Canada S4S 5W6
(306) 787-9034

Tourism Saskatchewan
1919 Saskatchewan Dr.
Regina, Saskatchewan
Canada S4P 3V7
(800) 667-7191

YUKON TERRITORY

**Dept. of Renewable Resources Fish
    and Wildlife Branch**
P.O. Box 2703
Whitehorse, Yukon Territory
Canada YlA 2C6
(403) 667-5811

Tourism Yukon
P.O. Box 2703
Whitehorse, Yukon Territory
Canada YlA 2C6
(403) 667-5340